Model Speeches for Practice

(美) Grenville Kleiser \著

海山 藕静清 \译

● 英汉对照

演讲的艺术

百花文艺出版社
BAIHUA LITERATURE AND ART PUBLISHING HOUSE

图书在版编目（CIP）数据

演讲的艺术：英汉对照/（美）克莱泽（Kleiser,G）著；海山，藕静清译. 一天津：百花文艺出版社，2009.1（2012.7重印）

ISBN 978-7-5306-5149-0

Ⅰ.演… Ⅱ.①克…②海…③藕… Ⅲ.演讲一语言艺术 Ⅳ.H019

中国版本图书馆CIP数据核字 (2009) 第000860号

百花文艺出版社出版发行

地址：天津市和平区西康路35号

邮编：300051

e-mail:bhpubl@public.tpt.tj.cn

http://www.bhpubl.com.cn

发行部电话：(022)23332651　邮购部电话：(022)27695043

全国新华书店经销

天津泰宇印务有限公司印刷

*

开本880×1230毫米　1/32　印张8.375　插页2　字数163千字

2009年4月第1版　2012年7月第3次印刷

印数：8001-11000册　　定价：18.00元

◉学习阐释思想的方法与技巧

◉品位千锤百炼的语言结晶

◉阅读高屋建瓴者的深邃思想

目录

Contents

前言

本书概括卓有成就的演讲者有代表性的各类成功演讲，为读者学习和训练口才提供了便利且有用的材料。

热切地建议学生每次选择一篇演讲词，仔细分析，体会其独具的特色，并大声诵读，然后再学习下一篇。这样学生便能全面了解演说的主要形式，并且能学以致用。

演讲者只有通过不断演讲才能提高演讲水平，这是最基本的规则。因此，仔细阅读、研习这些演讲对于提高学生的文学品位、培养他们良好的演说才能大有裨益。

格伦维尔·克莱泽

Preface

This book contains a varied representation of successful speeches by eminently successful speakers. They furnish, in convenient form, useful material for study and practise.

The student is earnestly recommended to select one speech at a time, analyze it carefully, note its special features, practise it aloud, and then proceed to another. In this way he will cover the principal forms of public speaking, and enable himself to apply his knowledge to any occasion.

The cardinal rule is that a speaker learns to speak by speaking, hence a careful reading and study of these speeches will do much to develop the student's taste for correct literary and oratorical form.

Grenville Kleiser

绪论

格伦维尔·克莱译

演讲的目的及意义

显然,演说的风格由你预期的目标来决定。如果你要宣扬重要的真理，或者致力于一项伟大而明确的事业，那么你的演讲可能会充满激情并极具说服力。

然而,如果你的演讲是出于自私的目的——为了自我宣传,或满足自己特殊的利益,如果你把演讲看成一件烦人的事情，或过于担心听众对你及你所付出努力的看法,那么你几乎注定要失败。

另一方面,如果你真诚地关心听众的利益,真正希望提供有益的公共服务——忘我地诚心服务于他人，那么你就具备了获得演讲真谛的最本质条件。

Introduction

Grenville Kleiser

Aims and Purposes of Speaking

It is obvious that the style of your public speaking will depend upon the specific purpose you have in view. If you have important truths which you wish to make known, or a great and definite cause to serve, you are likely to speak about it with earnestness and probably with eloquence.

If, however, your purpose in speaking is a selfish one—if your object is self-exploitation, or to serve some special interest of your own—if you regard your speaking as an irksome task, or are unduly anxious as to what your hearers will think of you and your effort—then you are almost sure to fail.

On the other hand, if you have the interests of your hearers sincerely at heart—if you really wish to render a worthy public service—if you lose all thought of self in your heartfelt desire to serve others——then you will have the most essential requirements of true and enduring oratory.

目标明确的必要性

对于演讲最终期望达到的目的要了然于胸，这一点至关重要。这一目标应该贯穿始终，这样你才能确保演讲的每一步都朝着预期的目标坚定地前进。

作为演讲者，你责任重大。不论好坏，你都会影响到别人。你所说的话就像无数的种子，种在听众的脑海里，在那里无论是“瓜”还是“豆”都会繁衍生长。你说的话可能会产生长远的影响，所以在规划和准备演讲时做到深思熟虑是十分重要的。

演讲的最高目标不仅仅是说教或娱乐，而是影响人们的意志，使他们与你产生思想共鸣，说服他们按照你的方式行事。一旦有正义事业作为后盾，这就是一个崇高的目标，值得你付出所有的才智和努力。

演讲成功的关键

卓越的演讲关键在于真挚。你自己必须让鞭策他人的话语符合真理和情理，这样才能使别人为你崇高的目标所打动。拥有他们的信任和祝福，你的演讲离成功已经咫尺之遥。

The Necessity of a Definite Object

It is of the highest importance for you to have in mind a clear conception of the end you wish to achieve by your speaking. This purpose should characterize all you say, so that at each step in your speech you will feel sure of making steady progress toward the desired object.

As a public speaker you assume serious responsibility. You are to influence men for weal or woe. The words you speak are like so many seeds, planted in the minds of your hearers, there to grow and multiply according to their kind. What you say may have far-reaching effects, hence the importance of careful forethought in the planning and preparation of your speeches.

The highest aim of your public speaking is not merely to instruct or entertain, but to influence the wills of men, to make men think as you think, and to persuade them to act in the manner you desire. This is a lofty aim, when supported by a good cause, and worthy of your greatest talents and efforts.

The Key to Success in Speaking

The key to greatness of speech is sincerity. You must yourself be so thoroughly imbued with the truth and desirability of what you are urging upon others that they will be impressed by your integrity of purpose. To have their confidence and good will is almost to win your cause.

但是你的演讲必须有说服力，因此论据也就必须要深刻而全面，这样才能期望说服并影响其他人。责任、需要、高尚、深信不疑和真心为他人谋福利的兴趣——这些才能产生真正的热忱，也是富有激情、充满说服力的演讲的精华。

利顿勋爵强调演讲者真诚的目标至关重要。提到英国国会的演讲，他说：“对你要说的主题拥有良好的感知和足够的知识，然后满怀诚意地用你自己真正的信念去感染其他人。无论你演讲的是什么，即使你的手势违反了昆体良提出的每一条规则，你也能使那些最有才华、最挑剔的人包括世界上最高贵的英国议会都竖起耳朵倾听，并影响他们的辩论。”

记住，你演讲的目的不仅仅是使听众相信你，而且还要说服他们。仅仅使他们同意你说的话还不够，必须说服他们按照你的要求去行动。

因此，你的目标应该是既抓住他们的思想又深入他们的内心。要达到第一个目标，需要可靠的论据、明确的方法和不可争辩的事实；而要实现第二个目标，则需要生动的想象、具体的说明和丰富的情感。

了解人性的必要

了解普通听众的品味、爱好、成见和癖性将有

But you must have deep and well-grounded convictions before you can hope to convince and influence other men. Duty, necessity, magnanimity, innate conviction, and sincere interest in the welfare of others,——these beget true fervor and are essential to passionate and persuasive speaking.

Lord Lytton emphasized the vital importance of earnest purpose in the speaker. Referring to speech in the British Parliament he said, "Have but fair sense and a competent knowledge of your subject, and then be thoroughly in earnest to impress your own honest conviction upon others, and no matter what your delivery, tho your gestures shock every rule in Quintilian, you will command the ear and influence the debates of the most accomplished, the most fastidious, and, take it altogether, the noblest assembly of freemen in the world."

Keep in mind that the purpose of your public speaking is not only to convince but also to persuade your hearers. It is not sufficient that they merely agree with what you say; you must persuade them also to act as you desire.

Hence you should aim to reach both their minds and hearts. Solid argument, clear method, and indisputable facts are necessary for the first purpose; vivid imagination, concrete illustration, and animated feeling are necessary for the second.

The Need of a Knowledge of Human Nature

It will be of great practical value to you to

很大的实用价值。你的演讲越能适应这些普通人，你就越可能成功地影响到所有听众。

所以，尽量使用你认为那些普通人容易理解的词、短语、例子和论据，避免使用任何可能引起他们困惑、心烦或偏见的词语。采用一切合理的方法赢得他们的好感和赞同。

演讲并不是独白，而是一种对话，在这个过程中，你是演讲者，而听众则是沉默而质疑的谛听者。他的脑子里时刻对你持有一种疑问的态度。你演讲的最后的成功将取决于你在多大程度上成功地回答了这些沉默而迫切的疑问。

使听者信服的过程主要依赖于先使自己信服。即便缺乏感情，你也许仍能在听众面前自圆其说，但是要想深入他们的内心，并确实达到预期的目标，就必须首先使自己感动。

作为演讲者，你的工作与演员或朗诵者有本质的差别，你不是模仿别人，也不是解说他人的思想。你首先必须自然、真实、诚挚、热切。你的工作是富有创造性和建设性的工作。

have a knowledge of the average man comprising your audience, his tastes, preferences, prejudices, and proclivities. The more you adapt your speech to such an average man, the more successful are you likely to be in influencing the entire audience.

Aim, therefore, to use words, phrases, illustrations, and arguments such as you think the average man will readily understand. Avoid anything which would cause confusion, distraction, or prejudice in his mind. Use every reasonable means to win his good will and approval.

Your speech is not a monolog, but a dialog, in which you are the speaker, and the auditor a silent tho questioning listener. His mind is in a constant attitude of interrogation toward you. And upon the degree of your success in answering such silent but insistent questions will depend the ultimate success of your speaking.

The process of persuading the hearer depends chiefly upon first being persuaded yourself. You may be devoid of feeling, and yet convince your hearers; but to reach their hearts and to move them surely toward the desired purpose, you must yourself be moved.

Your work as a public speaker is radically different from that of the actor or reciter. You are not impersonating some one else, nor interpreting the thought of another. You must above all things be natural, real, sincere and earnest. Your work is creative and constructive.

演讲者正确的态度

不管你学习、计划或事先考虑了多少，在对听众演讲时不能有任何故意做作的痕迹。那时，一切都必须与你的品格相吻合。

演讲的诚挚来源于你对瞄准的目标有清楚的构思，并且有一种实现它的强烈愿望。在这种情况下，你可以调动一切有用的思维和情感来助你一臂之力。你的心智能力被激发而进入最活跃状态，这样你就可以竭尽全力奔向前面的目标。

但是不管你对自己所拥护的事业的真理性和正义感有多么炽热，你最好还是经常把这种情感控制在适当的程度上为好。你可以充满活力却不可狂热，可以热情洋溢却不能夸大其词。

你不仅要充分了解自己以及演讲的主题，还必须熟知听众。你应该仔细思考出一种协调好自己与听众的最佳方法。可以通过倡导某种大家公认的原则，比如爱国主义、公平、人性、勇气、责任或正义来实现这种协调的状态。

菲利普·布鲁克斯说给传教士的话也同样适用于其他形式的演讲："布道中的一切都必须首先体现在传教士身上；头脑清楚、说话富于逻辑、活泼、热诚、和蔼以及有眼光都必须是他本人的品

The Right Attitude of a Speaker

However much you may study, plan, or premeditate, there must be no indication of conscious or studied attempt in the act of speaking to an audience. At that time everything must be merged into your personality.

Your earnestness in speaking arises principally from having a distinct conception of the object aimed at and a strong desire to accomplish it. Under these circumstances, you summon to your aid all your available power of thought and feeling. Your mental faculties are stimulated into their fullest activity, and you bend every effort toward the purpose before you.

But however zealous you may feel about the truth or righteousness of the cause you espouse, you will do well always to keep within the bounds of moderation. You can be vigorous without violence, and enthusiastic without extravagance.

You must not only thoroughly know yourself and your subject, but also your audience. You should carefully consider the best way to bring them and yourself into unity. You may do this by making an appeal to some principle commonly recognized and approved by men, such as patriotism, justice, humanity, courage, duty, or righteousness.

What Phillips Brooks said about the preacher, applies with equal truth to other forms of public speaking:" Whatever is in the sermon must be in the preacher first; clearness, logicalness, vivacity, earnestness, sweetness, and light, must be personal

质，然后才能成为他传达给教徒们的思想品质和语言风范。”

在认真学习了演讲的原理之后，你应该有计划地面对真实的听众经常进行定期练习。到处都有协会和社团不断地寻找优秀的演讲者，如果你的演讲能力已经达到一定水平，那么将有足够的机会等着你。

下面为你总结一些最基本的要点：

1. 每天大声朗读

这对于最大限度地提高你的演讲素养不可或缺。大声朗读,如果你认真去做的话,能迫使你读出所有单词,而不是像默读那样一掠而过。此外，它还有助于使你对于文章的韵律和结构得到一种有声的印象。

记住以下大声朗读的目的：

⑴ 提高讲话的音量。

⑵ 学会明确表达思想。

⑶ 培养准确发音。

⑷ 训练英式风格。

⑸ 增加单词储量。

⑹ 在脑子里储备论据。

⑺ 分析作者思想。

⑻ 扩充基础知识。

2. 养成记笔记的习惯

对于你很感兴趣并且打算日后进行演讲的题

qualities in him before they are qualities of thought and language in what he utters to his people."

After you have earnestly studied the principles of public speaking you should plan to have regular and frequent practise in addressing actual audiences. There are associations and societies everywhere, constantly in quest of good speakers. There will be ample opportunities for you if you have properly developed your speaking abilities.

And now to sum up some of the most essential things for you:

1. Read Aloud Every Day

This is indispensable to your greatest progress in speech culture. Reading aloud, properly done, compels you to pronounce the words, instead of skimming over them as in silent reading. It gives you the additional benefit of receiving a vocal impression of the rhythm and structure of the composition.

Keep in mind the following purposes of your reading aloud:

(1) To improve your speaking voice.

(2) To acquire distinct enunciation.

(3) To cultivate correct pronunciation.

(4) To develop English style.

(5) To increase your stock of words.

(6) To store your memory with facts.

(7) To analyze an author's thoughts.

(8) To broaden your general knowledge.

2. Form the Note-Book Habit

Keep separate note-books for the subjects in which you are deeply interested and on which you

目做分类笔记。在笔记本中把来源于观察、交谈、阅读和思考的任何有价值的观点立即记录下来。

用这种方式积累有用资料的速度之快会令你惊喜。在紧急情况下你可以求助于自己积累的演讲材料,及时解决“说什么”的问题。

保持笔记本内容的系统有序，将不同概念按照标题进行清晰地归类。如有可能,把自己的一些想法按正规演讲的格式写下来。每周大声朗读一次笔记本上的内容。

3. 每天研习字典

每天至少花五分钟大声诵读字典，特别要注意单词的读音和意义。这是积累大量词汇的最有效的方式之一。

养成查阅字典的习惯。对词汇要有兴趣。在上下文中学习单词。制定针对自己的单词列表。做到专词专用。泛读时记下重要的词汇。

词汇堪称演讲的重要工具。在日常谈话中要“咬文嚼字”，对于有疑问的词义及时查阅字典。做一个认真学习词汇的学生。

4. 系统地训练思维能力

每天花时间开发明辨是非的思维能力。学会

intend some time to speak in public. Write in them promptly any valuable ideas which come to you from the four principal sources—observation, conversation, reading, and meditation.

You will be surprized to find how rapidly you can acquire useful data in this way. In an emergency you can turn to the speech-material you have accumulated and quickly solve the problem of "what to say."

Keep the contents of your note-books in systematic order. Classify ideas under distinct headings. When possible write the ideas down in regular speech form. Once a week read aloud the contents of your note-books.

3. Daily Study Your Dictionary

Read aloud each day from your dictionary for at least five minutes, and give special attention to the pronunciation and meaning of words. This is one of the most useful exercises for building a large vocabulary.

Develop the dictionary habit. Be interested in words. Study them in their contexts. Make special lists of your own. Select special words for special uses. Note significant words in your general reading.

Think of words as important tools for public speaking. Choose them with discrimination in your daily conversation. Consult your dictionary for the meanings of words about which you are in doubt. Be an earnest student of words.

4. Systematically Develop Your Mental Powers

Give some time each day to the development of a judicial mind. Learn to think deliberately and

审慎并严谨地思考。研究事情的因果和规律。深入调查问题。

研究问题要公正无私。全面考虑问题的各个方面，本着查明事实真相的目的来权衡证据。

谨防偏见的影响，敞开心胸去接受各种事实。从他人的角度来看问题。培养思维的宽广。防止个人兴趣或想法让你误入歧途。坚持不惜一切代价维护真理。

5. 每天练习写作

经常动笔对提高演讲水平十分重要。每天写一点，以便养成英语的行文风格。每天练习写作将迅速提高演讲的准确性和流利性。

通过将重要观点写下来的方式对其进行检验。不断地培养表达的清晰度。检查、评论和修改自己的作文。

每天至少抄写一页有独特风格的大作家的作品，坚持练习一个月，你的演讲和写作将有明显进步。

6. 练习即兴演讲

每天在自己的房间里站起来至少作两到三分钟的即兴演讲。选择自己感兴趣的话题。目标在于培养风格的流畅而不在于思想的深度。

carefully. Study causes and principles. Look deeply into things.

Be impartial in your examination of a subject. Study all sides of a question or problem. Weigh the evidence with the purpose of ascertaining the truth.

Beware the peril of prejudice. Keep your mind wide open to receive the facts. Look at a subject from the other man's viewpoint. Cultivate breadth of mind. Do not let your personal interests or desires mislead you. Insist upon securing the truth at all costs.

5. Daily Practise Composition

Frequent use of the pen is essential to proficiency in speaking. Write a little every day to form your English style. Daily exercise in writing will rapidly develop felicity and fluency of speech.

Test your important ideas by putting them into writing. Constantly cultivate clearness of expression. Examine, criticize, and improve your own compositions.

Copy in your handwriting at least a page daily from one of the great English stylists. Continue this exercise for a month and note the improvement in your speech and writing.

6. Practise Impromptu Speaking

At least once a day stand up, in the privacy of your room, and make an impromptu speech of two or three minutes. Select any subject which interests you. Aim at fluency of style rather than depth of thought.

在日常练习时，要自觉地运用丹田发声，发音要清晰，嘴巴要张开，并想象自己确实在面对听众。这样定期练习一个月，你会对这种练习方式的重要性深信不疑。

7. 向成功的演讲者学习

尽可能听一些优秀演讲者的演讲。带着挑剔的眼光观察他们，同时问自己以下问题：

(1) 这位演讲者是如何给我留下深刻印象的？

(2) 他是否采用了最有效的方式进行演讲？

(3) 他是否使我相信他的叙述是真实的？

(4) 他是否说服了我按他所期望的那样去行动？

(5) 这位演讲者成功的要素是什么？

只要你切实地采用了以上种种建议，你的演讲艺术将得到不断的提高，你将学会运用这种有力的武器实现自我满足，更可以去激励自己同胞的胸怀，使他们也得到提高。

In these daily efforts, use the best chest voice at your command, enunciate clearly, open your mouth well, and imagine yourself addressing an actual audience. A month's regular practice of this exercise will convince you of its great value.

7. Study Successful Public Speakers

Hear the best public speakers available to you. Observe them critically. Ask yourself such questions as these:

(1) How does this speaker impress me?

(2) Does he proceed in the most effective manner possible?

(3) Does he convince me of the truth of his statements?

(4) Does he persuade me to act as he wishes?

(5) What are the elements of success in this speaker?

As you faithfully apply these various suggestions, you will constantly improve in the art of public speaking, and so learn to wield this mighty power not simply for your personal gratification but for the inspiration and betterment of your fellow men.

1.

晚宴后的演讲

詹姆斯·拉塞尔·洛威尔[1]

尊敬的科尔里奇勋爵，各位勋爵，
女士们，先生们：

我承认听了主人的祝酒词之后，我松了一口气，因为主人在祝酒词中告诉我们发言者可扮演的角色有三种：科学的角色、艺术的角色和此外的第三种角色。我看到科学与艺术已各有青睐的人选，那么我就只好选择第三种角色，信口开河地讲点儿其他话题啦。尊敬的勋爵，您已经提及晚宴后演讲的困难。我得说有些人晚宴演讲做得越多这种感觉就越强烈，我正是其中之一。演讲过程中有

[1]1819～1891，美国浪漫主义诗人，批评家，编辑，外交官。

1.

After-Dinner Speaking

By James Russell Lowell

My Lord Coleridge, My Lords,
Ladies and Gentlemen:

I confess that my mind was a little relieved when I found that the toast to which I am to respond rolled three gentlemen, Cerberus-like into one, and when I saw Science pulling impatiently at the leash on my left, and Art on my right, and that therefore the responsibility of only a third part of the acknowledgment has fallen to me. You, my lord, have alluded to the difficulties of after-dinner oratory. I must say that I am one of those who feel them more keenly the more after-dinner speeches I make. There are a great many

许多困难,而我认为有三个主要难题:第一是有太多话要说,结果话语争先恐后地脱口而出,压抑并蹂躏了语言的生命力;第二是尽管无话可说,听众却仍然期待着我们能填补他们思想的空白;第三个困难,我认为是最可怕的,那就是要在一位把你想说的话都说了、而且说得比你好的人之后作演讲,这就诱使我们和老语法学家一起高呼:“绞死这些家伙,他们抢先把我们的好话题都说完了!”

我们好几次间接提到7月4号这个日子,我相信在这个国庆纪念日,大家都认为每一个美国人都胸怀某种鸟类的精神——兼习纹章学的鸟类学家认为那鸟是展翅高飞的雄鹰(依我看只有他们这么认为)。这种精神促使每一个人,无论他愿意与否,为祖国大唱赞歌。我想说,这只是一种普遍的迷信,我希望能用寥寥数语在一定程度上改正它。我想问问各位,有没有其他任何一个民族将他们的民族自豪感局限于一年中的某一天来表达?请允许我谈谈我的一次亲身经历。很幸运我可以像尤利西斯一样到过许多城市,见过多种风土人情——也许比他还多。我观察到了一个常见的事实,那就是,加在所有美德前面的那些形容词,无一例外都是从地理上描述我所去的那个国家的。举个例子,我就不说具体名字了,假设我在小

difficulties in the way, and there are three principal ones, I think. The first is having too much to say, so that the words, hurrying to escape, bear down and trample out the life of each other. The second is when, having nothing to say, we are expected to fill a void in the minds of our hearers. And I think the third, and most formidable, is the necessity of following a speaker who is sure to say all the things you meant to say, and better than you, so that we are tempted to exclaim, with the old grammarian, "Hang these fellows, who have said all our good things before us!"

Now the Fourth of July has several times been alluded to, and I believe it is generally thought that on that anniversary the spirit of a certain bird known to heraldic ornithologists—and I believe to them alone—as the spread eagle, enters into every American's breast, and compels him, whether he will or no, to pour forth a flood of national self-laudation. This, I say, is the general superstition, and I hope that a few words of mine may serve in some sort to correct it. I ask you, if there is any other people who have confined their national self-laudation to one day in the year. I may be allowed to make one remark as a personal experience. Fortune had willed it that I should see as many—perhaps more—cities and manners of men as Ulysses; and I have observed one general fact, and that is, that the adjectival epithet which is prefixt to all the virtues is invariably the epithet which geographically describes the country that I am in. For instance, not to take any real name, if

人国，我会听到小人国的美德，比如小人国的勇气、常识,以及政治智慧。如果我跨过国界到了相邻的布鲁法斯卡共和国——自从斯威夫特时代起它就成了共和国——我听到上述所有的美德又突然变成布鲁法斯卡的美德了。

很高兴能借此机会向科尔里奇勋爵致谢,感谢他在这样一个场合将美国总统的名讳与女皇陛下的名讳相提并论（我相信这是第一次）。不论是他还是今晚各位贵宾所说的话都让我大为感动，其中有一个比较新的形容词反复出现,即“说英语的”一词。现在我们不断听到诸如“说英语的民族”、“说英语的人口”。我想这并不表示我们要忘记或者最好忘记“英国人”和“美国人”这些词所包含的民族竞争和民族自豪感，不过这个单词的确意味着在拥有共同祖先、使用同一种语言的所有人之间存在着一种永恒、持久的共鸣。尊敬的勋爵,您说我们的贵宾在美国将受到热烈欢迎,对此我确信不疑。他传承了一些从伯比奇时期到现在一代又一代活跃在英国舞台上的伟大演员的传统——应该说是高贵而卓越的风度，他作为演讲

I am in the kingdom of Lilliput, I hear of the Lilliputian virtues. I hear courage, I hear common sense, and I hear political wisdom called by that name. If I cross to the neighboring Republic Blefusca—for since Swift's time it has become a Republic—I hear all these virtues suddenly qualified as Blefuscan.

I am very glad to be able to thank Lord Coleridge for having, I believe for the first time, coupled the name of the President of the United States with that of her Majesty on an occasion like this. I was struck, both in what he said, and in what our distinguished guest of the evening said, with the frequent recurrence of an adjective which is comparatively new—I mean the word "English-speaking." We continually hear nowadays of the "English-speaking race," of the "English-speaking population." I think this implies, not that we are to forget, not that it would be well for us to forget, that national emulation and that national pride which is implied in the words "Englishman" and "American," but the word implies that there are certain perennial and abiding sympathies between all men of a common descent and a common language. I am sure, my lord, that all you said with regard to the welcome which our distinguished guest will receive in America is true. His eminent talents as an orator, the dignified—I may say the illustrious—manner in which he has sustained the traditions of that succession of great actors who, from the time of Burbage to his own, have illustrated the English stage, will be as highly

家的卓越才能在美国将会像在这儿一样备受推崇。

我相信英国的大法官也将受到美国法律界的欢迎（我自己尚无资格当律师），也许因为知道大法官先生并不是去当律师抢他们的饭碗的，他们会更加热情地欢迎他。很遗憾，他会发现美国法律由不戴英国传统假发的法官们来执行，不过我相信他会同样认为他们执行得很好。自从来到这儿，我就听到我的朋友们为此沉重哀叹，认为这一重要的革新一定预示着某种衰退。我用一个从父亲那儿听来的故事作为回答。父亲回忆起新英格兰最后一个继续戴假发的牧师，开始人们只是觉得异常，后来就觉得可恶了，最后这位牧师也不再戴了。然而他教区一位可怜的妇女却为此极度伤心，当牧师从教堂出来时，这位妇女半路截住他，说道："啊，尊敬的牧师，我过去听您的布道总是深受启迪，备感轻松，但是现在您不戴假发了，一切感觉都没有了。"在讲完这个宽慰的故事后，我觉得在英国朋友们的脸上看到了些许鼓励的表情。

但是我不能纵容自己说下去了。我敢肯定晚宴后的演讲中也有一种美德，那就是简洁，关于这一点我又想起了一个故事。大法官阁下已经告诉

appreciated there as here.

And I am sure that I may also say that the chief magistrate of England will be welcomed by the bar of the United States, of which I am an unworthy member, and perhaps will be all the more warmly welcomed that he does not come among them to practise. He will find American law administered—and I think he will agree with me in saying ably administered—by judges who, I am sorry to say, sit without the traditional wig of England. I have heard since I came here friends of mine gravely lament this as something prophetic of the decay which was sure to follow so serious an innovation. I answered with a little story which I remember having heard from my father. He remembered the last clergyman in New England who still continued to wear the wig. At first it became a singularity and at last a monstrosity; and the good doctor concluded to leave it off. But there was one poor woman among his parishioners who lamented this sadly, and waylaying the clergyman as he came out of church she said, "Oh, dear doctor, I have always listened to your sermon with the greatest edification and comfort, but now that the wig is gone all is gone." I have thought I have seen some signs of encouragement in the faces of my English friends after I have consoled them with this little story.

But I must not allow myself to indulge in any further remarks. There is one virtue, I am sure, in after-dinner oratory, and that is brevity; and as to that I am reminded of a story. The Lord Chief

过各位晚宴后演讲的组成部分，即笑话、引语，以及一些陈词滥调。我认为要想使陈词滥调出彩，就必须有非凡的才智。我想我还没有用过一个引语，现在我记起自己很小的时候听过的一件事——关于一个卫理公会教派牧师在美国的故事。有一次他在一个野营聚会上布道，讲的是约书亚奇迹。他是这样开始布道的："各位听众，太阳有三种运动：第一种是径直的，或者说顺行的运动；第二种是退后的，或者说逆行的运动；第三种就是我们经文中提到的：'太阳静止不动'"。

好了，各位先生，我不知道你们是否明白了故事的含义——我希望你们明白。晚宴后的演讲开头之后就直奔主题——这好比太阳的顺行运动。接着演讲者不再深入，开始重复自己的观点——这好比太阳的逆行运动。最后他有自知之明，结束演讲，这就是我前面提到的运动——太阳静止不动。

Justice has told you what are the ingredients of after-dinner oratory. They are the joke, the quotation, and the platitude; and the successful platitude, in my judgment, requires a very high order of genius. I believe that I have not given you a quotation, but I am reminded of something which I heard when very young—the story of a Methodist clergyman in America. He was preaching at a camp meeting, and he was preaching upon the miracle of Joshua, and he began his sermon with this sentence: "My hearers, there are three motions of the sun. The first is the straightforward or direct motion of the sun; the second is the retrograde or backward motion of the sun; and the third is the motion mentioned in our text—'the sun stood still.'"

Now, gentlemen, I don't know whether you see the application of the story—I hope you do. The after-dinner orator at first begins and goes straight forward—that is the straightforward motion of the sun. Next he goes back and begins to repeat himself—that is the backward motion of the sun. At last he has the good sense to bring himself to the end, and that is the motion mentioned in our text, as the sun stood still.

2.

英格兰——民族之母

拉尔夫·沃尔多·爱默生[①]

尊敬的主席，先生们：

很高兴与各位贵宾相聚在此，更荣幸地看到台上有这么多杰出人士的面孔。不过我早就认识这些人，还在家乡时，他们离我曾经很近，就像现在离你们很近一样。该社团及其领导人的论点为所有从事自由贸易的朋友们所熟知。《笨拙周报》上对娱乐活动和天才事迹的报道，政治、社会和大学校园的趣闻每半个月就会在波士顿和纽约的每一个男孩儿和女孩儿中传开。先生们，当我置身海上时，在船舱的桌子上发现了一本船长的“欧洲历史”——那就好像一份节目单或演出海报，向新英

①1803～1882，美国散文家，哲学家，诗人。

2.

England, Mother of Nations

By Ralph Waldo Emerson

Mr. Chairman and Gentlemen:

It is pleasant to me to meet this great and brilliant company, and doubly pleasant to see the faces of so many distinguished persons on this platform. But I have known all these persons already. When I was at home, they were as near to me as they are to you. The arguments of the League and its leader are known to all friends of free trade. The gaieties and genius, the political, the social, the parietal wit of "Punch" go duly every fortnight to every boy and girl in Boston and New York. Sir, when I came to sea, I found the "History of Europe" on the ship's cabin table, the property of the captain;—a sort of program or play-bill to tell the seafaring New Englander what

格兰海员说明如果在此登陆他们将发现什么。至于狄更斯笔下董贝的故事,先生们,凡是有纸张可供印刷的地方都能找到这本书;没有一个能够阅读的人不曾读过这本书;即使他不能阅读,他也会找一些慈善的人读给他听。

但这些本不应该由我来说。这些实实在在的赞美,若由能够更深刻体会并理解这些美德的人来说会更合适。我不是来此与各位说客套话的,而是来讨论一些我认为比赞美更吸引各位的事情。这些话无论是在工作日讲,还是在节假日讲,也无论是在本世纪说,还是留到下个世纪再说,都没有什么不合适的。让一位独居丛林中的美洲人想亲眼见见英格兰的正是撒克逊民族的道德特征——强烈的是非感,对撒克逊民族的爱和忠诚——这是帝国的特征,使他们志在拥有世界的统治权。正是这一点,奠定了那种贵族性格的基础,当然它会发生种种变异,因此人们常常看不见它的源头,可是一旦失去这源头,它也就垮掉了。在商店或修理厂,人们诚实地劳作,那种精确可靠的工作就是一种民族特点。这种道德良知是一个因素,另一个因素是贯穿各个阶层的那种忠诚的支持,那种友好的习性,那种人与人之间的相互尊敬——年复一

he shall find on landing here. And as for Dombey, sir, there is no land where paper exists to print on, where it is not found; no man who can read, that does not read it, and, if he can not, he finds some charitable pair of eyes that can, and hears it.

But these things are not for me to say; these compliments tho true, would better come from one who felt and understood these merits more. I am not here to exchange civilities with you, but rather to speak on that which I am sure interests these gentlemen more than their own praises; of that which is good in holidays and working-days, the same in one century and in another century. That which lures a solitary American in the woods with the wish to see England, is the moral peculiarity of the Saxon race,—its commanding sense of right and wrong,—the love and devotion to that,—this is the imperial trait, which arms them with the scepter of the globe. It is this which lies at the foundation of that aristocratic character, which certainly wanders into strange vagaries, so that its origin is often lost sight of, but which, if it should lose this, would find itself paralyzed; and in trade, and in the mechanic's shop, gives that honesty in performance, that thoroughness and solidity of work, which is a national characteristic. This conscience is one element, and the other is that loyal adhesion, that habit of friendship, that homage of man to man, running through all classes,—the electing of worthy persons to a certain fraternity, to acts of kindness and warm and staunch support, from year to year, from youth to

年，从年轻人到老人中选举出值得信赖的人来维系友爱，践行善良，热心并坚定地支持他们。这于给予和接受它的人们来说都一样可爱可敬。这与其他民族肤浅的情感、夸张的礼节和短暂的联系截然不同。

先生们，你们也许会认为我有些迂腐。虽然今天是节日，但我对任何节日都没有兴趣，除非它庆祝的是真正的而非虚伪的欢乐。现在是此地经济萧条、商业危机、人们饱受贫苦折磨的时候，鉴于此我想说，我认为你们不放弃举行文学庆典是正确的。我似乎听你们说过，无论发生什么，我们都不会少用一个花环或一束橄榄枝来装扮我们的年度盛典。因为我必须告诉各位，我年幼时就已知道自己祖先来自的不列颠岛并不是百花园，不是一年四季晴空朗朗、玫瑰盛开、音乐悠扬、欢歌笑语的天堂，相反，那是一个阴冷潮湿、雾霭重重、凄凄惨惨的国家。在那里，除了健硕的男人、善良的女人和一些品格坚定、忍耐力极强的人以外，一片荒芜；人们优异的品质慢慢显现；在争吵时你才会发现他们高尚的品德；他们不会一次袒露无疑；不论是亲密爱人还是冤家对头，只有长期接触才能逐渐了解他们，只有看到他们的行为才知道他们的优点；顺境中他们可能喜怒无常或郁郁寡欢，而一旦陷入逆境，他们将显示出无比的力量。

先生们，有位睿智的古人没有颂扬那艘彩旗

age,——which is alike lovely and honorable to those who render and those who receive it;——which stands in strong contrast with the superficial attachments of other races, their excessive courtesy, and short-lived connection.

You will think me very pedantic, gentlemen, but holiday tho it be, I have not the smallest interest in any holiday, except as it celebrates real and not pretended joys; and I think it just, in this time of gloom and commercial disaster, of affliction and beggary in these districts, that on these very accounts I speak of, you should not fail to keep your literary anniversary. I seem to hear you say that, for all that is come and gone, yet we will not reduce by one chaplet or one oak-leaf the braveries of our annual feast. For I must tell you, I was given to understand in my childhood that the British Island, from which my forefathers came, was no lotus-garden, no paradise of serene sky and roses and music and merriment all the year round, no, but a cold, foggy, mournful country, where nothing grew well in the open air, but robust men and virtuous women and these of a wonderful fiber and endurance; that their best parts were slowly revealed; their virtues did not come out until they quarrelled; they did not strike twelve the first time; good lovers, good haters, and you could know little about them till you had seen them long, and little good of them till you had seen them in action; that in prosperity they were moody and dumpish, but in adversity they were grand.

Is it not true, sir, that the wise ancients did not praise the ship parting with flying colors from

飘飘驶离港口的船，而只称颂那位衣衫褴褛、瘦骨嶙峋、旗帜破烂却历经风暴而返航的勇敢水手，这难道不对吗？因此，先生们，关于古老的英格兰，它既拥有财富、荣耀和战利品，又拥有上千年来积聚的弱点，无可救药地坚守着许多不能突然改变的古老传统，忍受着贸易的变迁以及无数新的生活方式、新建筑物、新艺术品、新机器和生存竞争的压力，可是我看到她并不沮丧，也不软弱，而是铭记着过去曾经历过的惨淡岁月。事实上，她在阴暗的日子里本能地看得更远，在战争与灾难的风暴中，她像大炮一样有一种神秘的活力和激情。我看到她即使是在暮年，也不衰败，而是青春洋溢，仍然敢于相信自己忍耐和发展的能力。鉴于此，我说：欢呼吧！民族之母，英雄之母，你的雄风依旧；你依然善于享受生活，你还能够及时找出对策，帮助人类实现当下最迫切的需要。因此，对于外国人，你总是一位好客的好主人，对于体贴、慷慨的英国人，你永远是他们真正的家园。就这样保持下去吧！保持下去吧！若非如此，若英格兰的勇气随这场商业危机而逝，我将回到马萨诸塞州的海角，或回到我自己的印第安小河旁，并且告诉我的同胞们，那个古老的民族一去不复返了，从此人类的坚韧和希望就只能存在于阿勒格尼山脉，他处则无迹可寻。

the port, but only that brave sailor which came back with torn sheets and battered sides, stript of her banners, but having ridden out the storm? And so, gentlemen, I feel in regard to this aged England, with the possessions, honors and trophies, and also with the infirmities of a thousand years gathering around her, irretrievably committed as she now is to many old customs which can not be suddenly changed; pressed upon by the transitions of trade, and new and all incalculable modes, fabrics, arts, machines and competing populations,—I see her not dispirited, not weak, but well remembering that she has seen dark days before; indeed with a kind of instinct that she sees a little better in a cloudy day, and that in storm of battle and calamity, she has a secret vigor and a pulse like a cannon. I see her in her old age, not decrepit, but young, and still daring to believe in her power of endurance and expansion. Seeing this, I say, All hail! mother of nations, mother of heroes, with strength still equal to the time; still wise to entertain and swift to execute the policy which the mind and heart of mankind require in the present hour, and thus only hospitable to the foreigner, and truly a home to the thoughtful and generous who are born in the soil. So be it! So be it! If it be not so, if the courage of England goes with the chances of a commercial crisis, I will go back to the capes of Massachusetts, and my own Indian stream, and say to my countrymen, the old race are all gone and the elasticity and hope of mankind must henceforth remain on the Alleghany ranges, or nowhere.

3.

探索的时代

威廉·尤尔特·格拉德斯通[1]

尊敬的主席、尊敬的殿下、阁下们、先生们：

我想关于在皇家学院祝酒名单中文学应位列其中这一正确的要求是毫无问题的。我参加过许多次热情洋溢的全委会，直到今天每一次我都怀着极大的满足感倾听着，但我必须说，从前没有任何安排比责成我向文学致谢更快乐、更使我满意的。然而，服从是我们必须遵守的准则，我至少还

①1809～1898，英国自由党议员，曾4次当选英国首相。

3.

The Age of Research

By William Ewart Gladstone

Mr. Chairman, Your Royal Highness,
My Lords and Gentlemen:

I think no question can be raised as to the just claims of literature to stand upon the list of toasts at the Royal Academy, and the sentiment is one to which, upon any one of the numerous occasions of my attendance at your hospitable board, I have always listened with the greatest satisfaction until the present day arrived, when I am bound to say that that satisfaction is extremely qualified by the arrangement less felicitous, I think, than any which preceded it that refers to me the duty of returning thanks for Literature. However, obedience is the principle upon which we must

有资格履行你们欣然交付我手中的职责——把积极持续的文学创作作为真正进步和人类幸福的基本条件，对于它的至关重要性，没有人比你们有更深更透的理解。现在每个人都会意识到，你所引用的诗人说过的姐妹情谊，是真正的姐妹情谊，因为文学和艺术都是美的忠实信徒。关于文学和艺术，我十分感激地说，在我周围并未发觉任何艺术要衰落的迹象，学院也没有任何衰败的迹象，当然，假如没人回应你对文学的敬意，那就应该另当别论了。

本世纪以来，全国的艺术家们都在为保持和提高他们的水平而孜孜不倦地努力，在这伟大的事业中，他们也许并没有经常获得来自周围流行的大众品味的支持。但是任何人，即使只是粗略地观赏一下装饰在这些墙上的作品，都会发现英国艺术仍然保持着创作的丰富性。在我的记忆中，今年在景区陈列室的作品和以往任何一年一样展示出了全面的优美风格以及同自然亲密而深刻的共鸣。

至于文学，任何一个正从生命的顶峰以不同速率衰退的人都会很自然地回忆往昔、展望未来。我们必须清楚，在这个国家以及其他国家，本世纪

proceed, and I have at least the qualification for discharging the duty you have been pleased to place in my hands—that no one has a deeper or more profound sense of the vital importance of the active and constant cultivation of letters as an essential condition of real progress and of the happiness of mankind, and here every one at once perceives that that sisterhood of which the poet spoke, whom you have quoted, is a real sisterhood, for literature and art are alike the votaries of beauty. Of these votaries I may thankfully say that as regards art I trace around me no signs of decay, and none in that estimation in which the Academy is held, unless to be sure, in the circumstance of your poverty of choice of one to reply to this toast.

During the present century the artists of this country have gallantly and nobly endeavored to maintain and to elevate their standard, and have not perhaps in that great task always received that assistance which could be desired from the public taste which prevails around them. But no one can examine even superficially the works which adorn these walls without perceiving that British art retains all its fertility of invention, and this year as much as in any year that I can remember, exhibits in the department of landscape, that fundamental condition of all excellence, intimate and profound sympathy with nature.

As regards literature one who is now beginning at any rate to descend the hill of life naturally looks backward as well as forward, and

前叶无疑将被未来视作辉煌的文学时代。我们中的长者曾经生活在许多伟人尚在世的年代，年轻人曾经听到老人们亲切地谈论到这些伟人并仍然拥有他们的作品，我相信这些作品将会继续为所有后人珍藏。假如我们希望文学仍然保持 1815 年和平之后第一个 50 年间那种高超卓绝的水平，那恐怕与前一段时间的实际情况不符。因为那 50 年是一个伟大的时期——是英国历史上伟大的时期，是德国历史上伟大的时期，是法国历史上伟大的时期，当然也是意大利历史上的伟大时期。

我说过，我们几乎不能期望文学继续保持那么完美的水平。毫无疑问，文学耕耘对这个国家的人们来说仍将十分重要，但是我们必须记住什么是文学和什么不是文学。首先，我们应该就编书不是文学达成共识。我不怀疑编书业会繁荣起来并逐年继续呈不断上升的趋势。但我们先暂且搁下它不谈。作为我个人，如果前瞻一点，我期待本世纪末期并不是严格意义上的纯文学时代——并不是以表现美为创作基本条件的大量优秀、不朽、壮

we must be becoming conscious that the early part of this century has witnessed in this and other countries what will be remembered in future times as a splendid literary age. The elder among us have lived in the lifetime of many great men who have passed to their rest—the younger have heard them familiarly spoken of and still have their works in their hands as I trust they will continue to be in the hands of all generations. I am afraid we can not hope for literature—it would be contrary to all the experience of former times were we to hope that it should be equally sustained at that extraordinarily high level which belongs, speaking roughly, to the first fifty years after the peace of 1815. That was a great period—a great period in England, a great period in Germany, a great period in France, and a great period, too, in Italy.

As I have said, I think we can hardly hope that it should continue on a perfect level at so high an elevation. Undoubtedly the cultivation of literature will ever be dear to the people of this country; but we must remember what is literature and what is not. In the first place we should be all agreed that bookmaking is not literature. The business of bookmaking I have no doubt may thrive and will be continued upon a constantly extending scale from year to year. But that we may put aside. For my own part if I am to look a little forward, what I anticipate for the remainder of the century is an age not so much of literature proper—not so much of great, permanent and splendid additions to those works in which beauty

丽的文学作品的时代，而是期待一个探索的时代。这是一个伟大的探索时代——对科学的伟大探索，对历史的伟大探索，无论给我们的民族还是给我们所居住的世界以启迪的一切领域都有所探索的时代；即使本世纪未来的那些岁月不会如以往那样灿烂辉煌，不能涌现许多伟大而不朽的作品，但可以期望它们仍能极大地丰富人类的知识；如果它们丰富了人类的知识，那么必然也为文学领域提供了奏响新乐章、创造新辉煌的素材。太阳有升有落。白天是阳光普照，夜晚则月色温柔，自然的重大变迁过程中也有停歇的时候。人类思想的一切重大飞跃也是如此。当我们仿佛看到重要、永恒的作品创作在减少时，请不要失望。我们的太阳只是暂时隐匿，就像弥尔顿笔下的启明星一样：

> 随后它抬起低垂的头，
> 重新发出明亮的光，
> 闪耀在凌晨的天空上。

我很高兴参加这样的盛会，它把全世界的注意力都吸引到文学与艺术以及文学与科学结合的

is embodied as an essential condition of production, but rather look forward to an age of research. This is an age of great research—of great research in science, great research in history—an age of research in all the branches of inquiry that throw light upon the former condition whether of our race, or of the world which it inhabits; and it may be hoped that, even if the remaining years of the century be not so brilliant as some of its former periods, in the production of works great in themselves, and immortal,—still they may add largely to the knowledge of mankind; and if they make such additions to the knowledge of mankind, they will be preparing the materials of a new tone and of new splendors in the realm of literature. There is a sunrise and sunset. There is a transition from the light of the sun to the gentler light of the moon. There is a rest in nature which seems necessary in all her great operations. And so with all the great operations of the human mind. But do not let us despond if we seem to see a diminished efficacy in the production of what is essentially and immortally great. Our sun is hidden only for a moment. It is like the day-star of Milton:

Which anon repairs his drooping head,
And tricks his beams, and with new spangled ore,
Flames in the forehead of the morning sky.

I rejoice in an occasion like this which draws the attention of the world to topics which illustrate

主题上来了。因为你们有很艰苦的路程要走，所以要坚决地抗拒身外之物的诱惑，不论这些诱惑表现的是追求钱财的机会还是寻求享乐的可能。你们有义务来告诫人们什么对人类最重要，即坚持这样的原则：只有平等、均衡并能开发我们天性中一切才能的进步才是真正的进步。如果一个国家的财富剧增，但那些增加的财富只是很大地刺激了奢侈的诞生，那么这种财富本身绝不能也永远不能称为进步。那只是一边倒的发展，是一种畸形的发展。我希望我们不会这样。避免畸形发展的一种方式就是宣扬各位今天维护的这种姐妹情谊论，而且我相信，只要有文人的地方，你们代表文学表达的良好愿望就能在艺术上引起共鸣。

the union of art with literature and of literature with science, because you have a hard race to run, you have a severe competition against the attraction of external pursuits, whether those pursuits take the form of business or pleasure. It is given to you to teach lessons of the utmost importance to mankind, in maintaining the principle that no progress can be real which is not equable, which is not proportionate, which does not develop all the faculties belonging to our nature. If a great increase of wealth in a country takes place, and with that increase of wealth a powerful stimulus to the invention of mere luxury, that, if it stands alone, is not, never can be, progress. It is only that one-sided development which is but one side of deformity. I hope we shall have no one-sided development. One mode of avoiding it is to teach the doctrine of that sisterhood you have asserted today, and confident I am that the good wishes you have exprest on behalf of literature will be re-echoed in behalf of art wherever men of letters are found.

4.

欢迎辞

奥利弗·温德尔·霍姆斯①

校友会的兄弟们:

今天由我代替要退休的老校长站在这里为大家做主持,这是你们的,也是我的一种不幸。也许你们不会相信, 我是多么地不情愿第二次站在这个尴尬的位置上,尽可能地代替老校长。他是那么风度翩翩、举止优雅,那么彬彬有礼、才华横溢,他在优秀的学子们中有极高的声望, 他既有资格指导学会,又能给节日盛会增辉。温斯罗普,这个名字早已和国家、大学紧密相连,置身于他温柔的羽翼下,就如同栖息于此处枝繁叶茂的大榆树下,其

①1841~1935,美国法学家,曾在美国最高法院任职30年。

4.

Address of Welcome

By Oliver Wendell Holmes

Brothers of the Association of the Alumni:

It is your misfortune and mine that you must accept my services as your presiding officer of the day in the place of your retiring president. I shall not be believed if I say how unwillingly it is that for the second time I find myself in this trying position; called upon to fill, as I best may, the place of one whose presence and bearing, whose courtesy, whose dignity, whose scholarship, whose standing among the distinguished children of the university, fit him alike to guide your councils and to grace your festivals. The name of Winthrop has been so long associated with the State and with the college that to sit under his mild empire is like

荫凉庇护的范围之广足以说明它的根扎入土壤的牢固程度。在国内动乱的岁月,我们这些祖国母亲的孩子,和睦地聚集在这里。当然此刻我们比以往任何时候都更加需要选个避难所，某个无暴力的圣堂来享受片刻的安宁，来逃避日常生活中的焦躁和忧虑。我们的生活由于兴奋而憔悴。战鼓的雷鸣,步兵的行军,骑兵的疾驰,炮火的咆哮,无论醒着还是睡着,白天还是黑夜,这些声音无时无刻不响彻在我们的耳边。而这样的情况已经持续两年多了。我们鲜有人不曾发抖和战栗,因为我们时常要为自己所爱的人们担心。哎呀,多少人曾听到我为逝者哀悼——他们虽然离开了尘世，他们的精神却在国家的荣誉和我们的爱中永存！我们需要一点呼吸的空间来抛弃焦虑的情绪，来梦想美好的未来——就像日后 我们也会回顾起在这座安宁的避难所度过的平静的日子一样。 当上帝完成了自己的睿智目标后，那久别我们的美丽天使就会将其圣手放在我们这个战乱不已的民族的心上,轻声说:“和平！安静吧！”

这里，恐怕是世界上我们最有希望找到和平的地方。在新英格兰,仅存的净土似乎便是那一处处老墓地,还有这些大树环绕、可亲可爱的旧校舍

resting beneath one of these wide–branching elms the breadth of whose shade is only a measure of the hold its roots have taken in the soil. In the midst of civil strife we, the children of this our common mother, have come together in peace. And surely there never was a time when we more needed a brief respite in some chosen place of refuge, some unviolated sanctuary, from the cares and anxieties of our daily existence than at this very hour. Our life has grown haggard with excitement. The rattle of drums, the march of regiments, the gallop of squadrons, the roar of artillery, seem to have been continually sounding in our ears day and night, sleeping and waking, for two long years and more. How few of us have not trembled and shuddered with fear over and over again for those whom we love. Alas! How many that hear me have mourned over the lost—lost to earthly sight, but immortal in our love and their country's honor! We need a little breathing–space to rest from our anxious thoughts, and, as we look back to the tranquil days we passed in this still retreat, to dream of that future when in God's good time, and after his wise purpose is fulfilled, the fair angel who has so long left us shall lay her hand upon the leaping heart of this embattled nation and whisper, "Peace! be still!"

Here of all places in the world we may best hope to find the peace we seek for. It seems as if nothing were left undisturbed in New England except here and there an old graveyard, and these dear old College buildings, with the trees in which

了。旧议会大楼里挤满了卖牛羊、鸽子和兑换钱币的小贩。而汉考克宫——这个连接城市与历史的脐带，正如同水中涟漪一般在逐渐消失。

但是马萨诸塞州——德高望重的马萨诸塞州，依然稳固坚定。霍利斯厅，到今年已经是百年老舍了，它正满面红光、热情真挚地期待着欢迎第一百代校友；霍尔登教堂拥有华丽的多利斯式壁缘，大门上镶有天真无邪的小天使，它安静地凝视着落日。我们聚集于哈佛古老的围墙之内，这里的晨钟唤醒过无数困倦的少年。此刻它正坚守岗位，准备将那些新生羽翼的大学新生从不安的第一夜惊起。当我们的父辈年幼时，当我们自己还是孩子的时候，所有这些受人敬仰的建筑就如同现在一样屹然矗立。不要让那些轻率鲁莽的修缮之手毁坏了它们的圣洁，因为这些砌墙的水泥并不是什么劣质的灰浆，而是由那比墙连成的建筑更为坚固的情谊和记忆调和而成的。

我们忘记了所有微小的差异，在这良辰相遇。跨入神圣的校园时，我们将在校门口脱掉象征着各自宗教和政治派别的制服，换上由高贵的女王亲自订制的宫廷礼服，那是过去的70年中我们所穿的校服。我们永远不会忘记老校友们自从

they are embowered. The old State House is filled with those that sell oxen and sheep and doves, and the changers of money. The Hancock house, the umbilical scar of the cord that held our city to the past, is vanishing like a dimple from the water.

But Massachusetts, venerable old Massachusetts, stands as firm as ever; Hollis, this very year a centenarian, is waiting with its honest red face in a glow of cordiality to welcome its hundredth set of inmates; Holden Chapel, with the skulls of its Doric frieze and the unpunishable cherub over its portals, looks serenely to the sunsets; Harvard, within whose ancient walls we are gathered, and whose morning bell has murdered sleep for so many generations of drowsy adolescents, is at its post, ready to startle the new-fledged freshmen from their first uneasy slumbers. All these venerable edifices stand as they did when we were boys,—when our grandfathers were boys. Let not the rash hand of innovation violate their sanctities, for the cement that knits these walls is no vulgar mortar, but is tempered with associations and memories which are stronger than the parts they bind together!

We meet on this auspicious morning forgetting all our lesser differences. As we enter these consecrated precincts, the livery of our special tribe in creed and in politics is taken from us at the door, and we put on the court dress of our gracious Queen's own ordering, the academic robe, such as we wore in those bygone years scattered along the seven last decades. We are not forgetful

接受大学教育后所取得的荣耀——他们的演说，论文，专论，著作和希腊语对话作品。但是今天我们不分等级，我们都是一流的学者。头戴桂冠的英雄邻座是颈下干花花环发出美妙窸窣声的博士，而头戴月桂冠的诗人和头戴常春藤冠的批评家手握着手，大家是同一个快乐大家庭的成员。这是一个生日盛会，属于我们每一个受过刻着“基督教会众”字样的圣盆洗礼的人。我们没有奖章只有毕业证，没有荣誉称号只有毕业的届次。这是共和精神在大学里的体现。在这个伟大的集体中，我们所有的人天生都是平等的。

欢迎，欢迎你们，我亲爱的同学们，欢迎来到这个愉快的盛会！尽管有一些悲伤的思绪，我们仍然要称之为愉快的盛会！我们上一回每三年一次的盛会有着双重意义，因为那一天我们聚集在一起还有另外一个原因，那就是我们大学古老的“大家庭”来了一位新校长。今天，未能再见到他魁梧的身影和亲切的微笑，这使我不由得想起以前一位大学校长在悼念友人时的一段感人的话语。那是在1678年的毕业典礼仪式上，敬爱的尤里安·奥克斯校长追悼查尔斯顿的牧师，也是我们大学的督导——托马斯·谢泼德时所讲的话：“与我友

of the honors which our fellow students have won since they received their college "parts,"—their orations, dissertations, disquisitions, colloquies, and Greek dialogs. But today we have no rank; we are all first scholars. The hero in his laurels sits next to the divine rustling in the dry garlands of his doctorate. The poet in his crown of bays, the critic, in his wreath of ivy, clasp each other's hands, members of the same happy family. This is the birthday feast for every one of us whose forehead has been sprinkled from the font inscribed "Christo et Ecclesioe." We have no badges but our diplomas, no distinctions but our years of graduation. This is the republic carried into the university; all of us are born equal into this great fraternity.

Welcome, then, welcome, all of you, dear brothers, to this our joyous meeting! We must, we will call it joyous, tho it comes with many saddening thoughts. Our last triennial meeting was a festival in a double sense, for the same day that brought us together at our family gathering gave a new head to our ancient household of the university. As I look today in vain for his stately presence and kindly smile, I am reminded of the touching words spoken by an early president of the university in the remembrance of a loss not unlike our own. It was at the commencement exercises of the year 1678 that the Reverend President Urian Oakes thus mourned for his friend Thomas Shepard, the minister of Charlestown, an overseer of the college: "*Dici non potest quam me*

相见总是让我感到既轻松又愉快。然而如今他却永远离开了我们，我再也看不到他的身影了。”（拉丁文）说这些话的是我校的第四任校长，距今日已近二百年，而我将上述话语用来悼念我们的第20任校长却再合适不过了。这位杰出而成熟的学者忽然离我们而去，这就如同满载货物的大货船刚刚抵达港口，就在青天白日里带着全部宝贵的财富坠入了海底。

我们现在正经受着战乱，在今天这样的场合，每一个敬爱的名字都会勾起我们的回忆，而伤痛几乎成了我们的常客。许多孩子接受了祖国所教授的文化知识，却将青春的朝气和男儿的力量都献给了战争。最近“身佩星形勋章的人已经与生者阴阳两隔”（拉丁文）多么频繁地被诠释成标语！仿佛这个战乱的红色星球已经取代了那个和平的星球。这些名单印有一大长串我们大学毕业的烈士的名字，红成一片。我不想唱颂歌，因为我的字典里已经没有词汇适于把他——基督的卫士珍藏

perorantem, in comitiis, conspectus ejus, multo jucundissimus, recrearit et refecerit. At non comparet hodie Shepardus in his comitiis; oculos huc illuc torqueo; quocumque tamen inciderint, Platonem meum intanta virorum illustrium frequentia requirunt; nusquam amicum et pernecessarium meum in hac solenni panegyric, inter nosce Reverendos Theologos, Academiae Curatores, reperire aut oculis vestigare possum." Almost two hundred years have gone by since these words were uttered by the fourth president of the college, which I repeat as no unfitting tribute to the memory of the twentieth, the rare and fully ripened scholar who was suddenly ravished from us as some richly freighted argosy that just reaches her harbor and sinks under a cloudless sky with all her precious treasures.

But the great conflict through which we are passing has made sorrow too frequent a guest for us to linger on an occasion like this over every beloved name which the day recalls to our memory. Many of the children whom our mother had trained to arts have given the freshness of their youth or the strength of their manhood to arms. How strangely frequent in our recent record is the sign interpreted by the words "E vivis cesserunt stelligeri!" It seems as if the red war-planet had replaced the peaceful star, and these pages blushed like a rubric with the long list of the martyr-children of our university. I can not speak their eulogy, for there are no phrases in my vocabulary fit to enshrine the memory of the Christian

在记忆中：

他注定与痛苦、恐惧
和流血为伴，悲惨的列车
把他的命运变成辉煌的收获——
无论是否受到称赞，他都必须
永远跋涉，在四方立下崇高的功绩。
要么他就默默无闻地倒下长眠
只留下一个无益无用的名字，
可是他能在自己的事业中自寻慰藉；
当致命的雾霭渐渐聚拢时，
他会因坚信天堂的掌声而感到欣慰。

兄弟们，我想再一次重申，现在还不是悲伤的时候。时光荏苒，转眼间月变成年，我们向着站在城墙上的人哭喊："守卫，黑夜还有多久？"他们一遍一遍地回答："天色已经在破晓，白天马上就要到来。"但是黑夜却更加黑暗了。最终——啊，我的上帝——最终我们无需守卫们的消息，因为无论是东方还是西方的地平线上都迸射出一片灿烂的光辉，那是胜利的红色曙光！

今天我们没有举办舞会，然而当共和国胜利的旗帜把溃退的敌人追到愤怒的波托马克河岸边时，哪个人的胸中不悸动着喜悦？共和国诞生的那个早上，伴随着哈得孙港内坚固鹿砦内传出的北方军团晨起的号声，西军蜂拥冲进了沦陷的威克

warrior,—of him—

Who, doomed to go in company with Pain
And Fear and Bloodshed, miserable train,
Turns his necessity to glorious gain—
Who, whether praise of him must walk the earth
Forever, and to noble deeds give birth,
Or he must fall, to sleep without his fame,
And leave a dead, unprofitable name,
Finds comfort in himself and in his cause;
And while the mortal mist is gathering, draws
His breath in confidence of Heaven´s applause.

Yet again, O brothers! This is not the hour for sorrow. Month after month until the months became years we have cried to those who stood upon our walls: "Watchmen, what of the night?" They have answered again and again, "The dawn is breaking,—it will soon be day." But the night has gathered round us darker than before. At last—glory be to God in the highest!—at last we ask no more tidings of the watchmen, for over both horizons east and west bursts forth in one overflowing tide of radiance the ruddy light of victory!

We have no parties here today, but is there one breast that does not throb with joy as the banners of the conquering Republic follow her retreating foes to the banks of the angry Potomac? Is there one heart that does not thrill in answer to the drum-beat that rings all over the world as the army of the west, on the morning of the nation´s

斯堡寂静沉闷的工事，当听到那响彻云霄的战鼓声，哪个人的心会不为之震颤呢？我们是学者，我们是毕业生，我们是校友，我们是一帮兄弟，除此之外，最重要的，我们是美国公民。既然希望在我们这块土地上已经破晓——不，已经迸射出巨大的光辉——难道我们没有感受到这道光芒？尽管在战乱中，可我们仍能和平地团聚，这是因为我们人民的战士有力的手已经将战乱扼住。

欢迎你们，非常的欢迎，我的学术战士，你们曾为你们和我们的权利和荣誉而战！欢迎你们，军中学者，你们时刻准备着祖国的召唤，准备着去战斗！欢迎你们，你们既宣扬温顺又宣扬勇敢，你们没忘记和平王子也佩戴着剑！欢迎你们，你们制定和解读法规，旨在和平中捍卫自由而不是在战争中帮助敌人！欢迎你们，你们的健康服务用高超的救护技术和温柔的安慰抚平了患病和病危的人们的痛苦！欢迎你们，你们正在培育我们慷慨的年轻人，祖国期盼他们成为未来的卫士！欢迎你们，寡言的学者们，你们在寂寞中研究学问，不知不觉地塑造着思想，那思想将会被铸入法律坚实的盾牌，成为战争中电闪雷鸣般的武器！

对于您，校长先生，我们将您从充满信任与光荣的地方请来，来领导这个古老而崇高的大学。我

birth, swarms over the silent, sullen earthworks of captured Vicksburg,—to the reveille that calls up our Northern regiments this morning inside the fatal abatis of Port Hudson? We are scholars, we are graduates, we are alumni, we are a band of brothers, but beside all, above all, we are American citizens. And now that hope dawns upon our land—nay, bursts upon it in a flood of glory,—shall we not feel its splendors reflected upon our peaceful gathering, peaceful in spite of those disturbances which the strong hand of our citizen-soldiery has already strangled?

Welcome then, thrice welcome, scholarly soldiers who have fought for your and our rights and honor! Welcome, soldierly scholars who are ready to fight whenever your country calls for your services! Welcome, ye who preach courage as well as meekness, remembering that the Prince of Peace came also bringing a sword! Welcome, ye who make and who interpret the statutes which are meant to guard our liberties in peace, but not to aid our foes in war! Welcome, ye whose healing ministry soothes the anguish of the suffering and the dying with every aid of art and the tender accents of compassion! Welcome, ye who are training the generous youths to whom our country looks as its future guardians! Welcome, ye quiet scholars who in your lonely studies are unconsciously shaping the thought which law shall forge into its shield and war shall wield as its thunder-bolt!

And to you, Mr. President, called from one

们向您致以最热烈的欢迎，希望并祝愿您在这里长久而快乐地任职。

兄弟们，校友联盟的兄弟们，这些孩子已经认定伟大母亲为他们细心挑选的新父亲了，下面有请他对我们庞大的家族说几句吧。

注：在坎布里奇校友会晚宴上的演讲词。

place of trust and honor to rule over the concerns of this our ancient and venerated institution, to you we offer our most cordial welcome with all our hopes and prayers for your long and happy administration.

I give you, brothers, "The association of the Alumni"; the children of our common mother recognize the man of her choice as their new father, and would like to hear him address a few words to his numerous family.

FOOTNOTE:
Delivered at an Alumni Dinner, Cambridge.

5.

祝福美国

威廉·哈考特爵士[①]

先生们：

尽管我意识到自己不够资格出席这次非凡的聚会并受到青睐，但我还是毫不犹豫地答应了这个刚刚收到的邀请，来履行一个对我来说不胜荣幸、对大家来说也很愉快的义务——那就是提议大会将谢意表达给主席先生，感谢他今日给我们的主持。我们今天在这个场合相聚向卡里森先生表示敬意，是因为每个人都仰慕他的人品，同时也一定感觉到今天主持的人选是恰得其人、独一无

①1827～1904，英国自由党议员，律师，记者。

5.

Good Will to America

By Sir William Harcourt

Gentlemen:

Small as are the pretensions which, on any account, I can have to present myself to the attention of this remarkable assemblage, I have had no hesitation in answering the call which is just been made upon me by discharging a duty which is no less gratifying to me than I know it will be agreeable to you—that of proposing that the thanks of this meeting be offered to the chairman for his presidence over us today. Every one who admires Mr. Garrison for the qualities on account of which we have met to do him honor on this occasion, must feel that there is a singular appropriateness in the selection of the person who has presided here

二的。没有人不会注意到这两位杰出人物事业上那惊人的相似之处，我几乎可以说是真正同样的伟大。两个人都凭着崇高的思想和激励自己前进的不屈不挠的正义精神，非凡地推进了真理事业，并维护了人权。而且两个人都足够幸运地在有生之年看到自己为倡导伟大目标所做的努力获得了期望中的巨大成功，也可以说远远超越了他们的希望。任何与布赖特先生名字相联系的事业都最终走向了胜利。

我不想重复前面的演讲者已经精辟论述过的话题。尽管今天有许多更有才能的演讲者已经解读了你们的愿望与梦想，但是请允许我加入到人们已经发出的支持英国和美国永久和睦的呼声中。我个人认为，无论是国家还是个人，性格的伟大主要依赖于能够带着希望和信念站在现在低级、狭隘和微小的利益之上期盼伟大未来的程度。我要问，哪里能找到我们民族的未来呢？我还可以接着问——哪里能找到人类的未来呢？答案并不

today. No one can fail to perceive a striking similarity—I might almost say a real parallelism of greatness—in the careers of these two eminent persons. Both are men who, by the great qualities of their minds, and the uncompromising spirit of justice which has animated them, have signally advanced the cause of truth and vindicated the rights of humanity. Both have been fortunate enough in the span of their own lifetime to have seen their efforts in the promotion of great ends crowned by triumphs as great as they could have desired, and far greater than they could have hoped. There is no cause with which the name of Mr. Bright has been associated which has not sooner or later won its way to victory.

I shall not go over the ground which has been so well dealt with by those who have preceded me. But tho there have been many abler interpreters of your wishes and aspirations today than I can hope to be, may I be permitted to join my voice to those which have been raised up in favor of the perpetual amity of England and America. It seems to me that with nations, as well as with individuals, greatness of character depends chiefly on the degree in which they are capable of rising above thee low, narrow, paltry interests of the present, and of looking forward with hope and with faith into the distance of a great futurity. And where, I will ask, is the future of our race to be found? I may extend the question—where is to be found the future of mankind? Who that can forecast the fortunes of the ages to come will not

在预知时代兴衰的先知那里——而就在伟大的民族身上，这民族是我们亲生的孩子，是我们的亲骨肉。历史的更迭充满着灭亡的王国和消失的种族的残骸。亚述国、埃及、希腊文明和庞大的罗马帝国都哪儿去了？他们征服其他的国家建立了王朝，却毁灭于自己赖以崛起的刀剑之下。我们的命运也会和他们的一样吗？我希望不是的——我相信不是。但是假如我们衰落的那天万一到来的话，至少我们会心存慰藉，因为我们知道我们已经留下了一个铭记我们的名字并将重塑我们的伟业的民族。历史上还有比我们有更合理的理由为自己的子孙感到骄傲的父母吗？还有比我们更有理由对自己的父辈心存感激的子孙吗？美国的自由制度，政府职能和成就伟业的能力不正是与我们一脉相承的吗？而恰恰是这些造就了美国的今天也保证了她的明天。这些很值得我们去铭记、去思考。因此，就如同我们这位生性谦虚的贵客所言，这不仅仅是私人庆宴，也绝不是逢场作戏的恭维。我们看到了其更深更广的意义，我们可以借此欢庆两国的团结友谊。在我要求大家向我们的主席表示谢意的同时，我也斗胆向我们的客人提出另一个请求，我想他是不会拒绝的。我们有个重要的口信要送出去，而眼下刚好有位带这个口信的合适的信

answer—it is in that great nation which has sprung from our loins, which is flesh of our flesh and bone of our bone. The stratifications of history are full of the skeletons of ruined kingdoms and of races that are no more. Where are Assyria and Egypt, the civilization of Greece, the universal dominion of Rome? They founded empires of conquest, which have perished by the sword by which they rose. Is it to be with us as with them? I hope not—I think not. But if the day of our decline should arise, we shall at least have the consolation of knowing that we have left behind us a race which shall perpetuate our name and reproduce our greatness. Was there ever parent who had juster reason to be proud of its offspring? Was there ever child that had more cause for gratitude to its progenitor? From whom but us did America derive those institutions of liberty, those instincts of government, that capacity of greatness, which have made her what she is, and which will yet make her that which she is destined to become? These are things which it becomes us both to remember and to think upon. And, therefore, it is that, as our distinguished guest, with innate modesty, has already said, this is not a mere personal festivity—this is no occasional compliment. We see in it a deeper and wider significance. We celebrate in it the union of two nations. While I ask you to return your thanks to our chairman I think I may venture also to ask of our guest a boon which he will not refuse us. We have a great message to send, and we have here a messenger

使。我将请求卡里森先生将这次聚会和这个国家的祝愿带回他的故乡，祝福英美两国永远和平、永远友好。因为美国和英国的友好不啻为自由与和平的福音。又有谁比今天我要求你们致以谢意的主席先生，更有资格主持这次福音的聚会呢？我恳请大会将掌声献给布赖特先生。

注：在伦敦为卡里森先生举办的早餐会上的演讲。

worthy to bear it. I will ask Mr. Garrison to carry back to his home the prayer of this assembly and of this nation that there may be forever and forever peace and good will between England and America. For the good will of America and England is nothing less than the evangel of liberty and of peace. And who more worthy to preside over such a gospel than the chairman to whom I ask you to return your thanks today? I beg to propose that the thanks of the meeting be given to Mr. Bright.

FOOTNOTE:
Speech at breakfast held in London in honor of Mr. Garrison.

6.

获胜的品质

查尔斯·萨姆纳[1]

尊敬的总统先生，新英格兰的同学们：

这是我有生以来第一次有幸参加这个闻名的周年纪念。尽管我常常荣幸地收到您诱人的邀请，也渴望来参加这名人云集的盛大聚会，却又总是不能从另一地方的工作中脱身。如果说我现在抵御不住众所周知的诱惑，首次从华盛顿长期的公务中脱身来旅行度假，那是因为你们优秀总统的感染力给这一切又平添了魅力。我们在波士顿、纽约和国外多年的友谊让我一定要来见他。我们不

① 1811～1874，美国政治家。

6.

The Qualities That Win

By Charles Sumner

Mr. President and Brothers of New England:

For the first time in my life I have the good fortune to enjoy this famous anniversary festival. Tho often honored by your most tempting invitation, and longing to celebrate the day in this goodly company of which all have heard so much, I could never excuse myself from duties in another place. If now I yield to well-known attractions, and journey from Washington for my first holiday during a protracted public service, it is because all was enhanced by the appeal of your excellent president, to whom I am bound by the friendship of many years in Boston, in New York, and in a foreign land. It is much to be a brother of New

仅是新英格兰的兄弟，更是朋友，我很高兴今晚能说明这种关系。

带着诸多的谦恭和疑虑，我斗胆代美国参议院致答，恐怕我的莽撞之言不会是最谨慎的。但是我却可以十分肯定地说任何一个参议员对出席这个盛大宴会都会感到高兴。什么是参议院呢？它是国家政府的一个组成部分。但是我们今天为之庆祝的不是任何一个政府的任何一个组织。我们庆祝的是人类历史上的一个纪元，这个纪元不仅永远不会被忘记，而且随着世界对真正伟大的东西的赏识，它会越来越辉煌。在人类历史上，1620 年 12 月 22 日英国清教徒登上普利茅斯海岸巨砾标志着一个新时代的开始，那是一个令全人类崛起的时代，那一刻是一个伟大的开端。

纵观历史，从远古时起，人们就一直在拥入偏僻的地方建立新的家园。推罗人先是沿着北非海岸跋涉而后驻足在迦太基；迦太基人后来又散布在西班牙，甚至散布在遥远的英国和爱尔兰的海滨地区；希腊人用热爱艺术的村落点缀着意大利和西西里；罗马似善战的雄鹰一般征服了众多殖民地。撒克逊人、斯堪的纳维亚人和诺曼人强行吞并了原始的布立吞人。而在现代，威尼斯、热那亚、葡萄牙、西班牙、法国和英国都曾派遣移民居住在

England, but it is more to be a friend, and this tie I have pleasure in confessing tonight.

It is with much doubt and humility that I venture to answer for the Senate of the United States, and I believe the least I say on this head will be the most prudent. But I shall be entirely safe in expressing my doubt if there is a single Senator who would not be glad of a seat at this generous banquet. What is the Senate? It is a component part of the National Government. But we celebrate today more than any component part of any government. We celebrate an epoch in the history of mankind—not only never to be forgotten, but to grow in grandeur as the world appreciates the elements of true greatness. Of mankind I say—for the landing on Plymouth Rock, on December 22, 1620, marks the origin of a new order of ages, which the whole human family will be elevated. Then and there was the great beginning.

Throughout all time, from the dawn of history, men have swarmed to found new homes in distant lands. The Tyrians, skirting Northern Africa, stopt at Carthage; Carthaginians dotted Spain and even the distant coasts of Britain and Ireland; Greeks gemmed Italy and Sicily with art-loving settlements; Rome carried multitudinous colonies with her conquering eagles. Saxons, Danes, and Normans violently mingled with the original Britons. And in modern times, Venice, Genoa, Portugal, Spain, France, and England, all sent forth emigrants to people foreign shores. But in these

国外。但是在这些各种各样的远征中，贸易或战争是行动的有力动机。贸易和征服常常并肩前行，鲜血染红了殖民地。

在我们所纪念的这一天，太阳第一次在其运行中俯视着一派不同的景象，这种景象始于一种新的精神，并将因此而持续下去。一些有良知的英国人顺从心中的意愿，要按照自己的意志自由地崇拜上帝，于是便起航去探索北美大陆的未知的荒野。他们靠着自由在船头、良知在舵柄的五月花号船，经过64天的航程，终于看到了科德角的白色沙滩，紧接着便在那小小的船舱里草拟了那一份永垂千古的简短契约，这是人类史上第一份成文的政体章程，是美利坚共和政体的奠基石。随后这些前辈移民便上了岸。

这份契约不仅在时间上是最早的，而且具有庄严的特征，堪称不朽的经典。在这之前还从来没有"一伙民众"宣布自己的目标是"不时地制定、通过、颁布最能满足和方便殖民地大众利益的公正、公平的法律、法令、法案、宪法和公职职责。"多么高尚！多么真实！毫无疑问，这是那个时代所能听到的政府最豪迈的话语和最伟大的承诺。

如果需要更多话语来描绘这个新纪元，我们

various expeditions, trade or war was the impelling motive. Too often commerce and conquest moved hand in hand, and the colony was incarnadined with blood.

On the day we celebrate, the sun for the first time in his course looked down upon a different scene, begun and continued under a different inspiration. A few conscientious Englishmen, in obedience to the monitor within, and that they might be free to worship God according to their own sense of duty, set sail for the unknown wilds of the North American continent. After a voyage of sixty-four days in the ship *Mayflower*, with Liberty at the prow and Conscience at the helm, they sighted the white sandbanks of Cape Cod, and soon thereafter in the small cabin framed that brief compact, forever memorable, which is the first written constitution of government in human history, and the very corner-stone of the American Republic; and then these Pilgrims landed.

This compact was not only foremost in time, it was also august in character, and worthy of perpetual example. Never before had the object of the "civil body public" been announced as "to enact, constitute, and frame such just and equal laws, ordinances, acts, constitutions, and offices from time to time as shall be thought most meet and convenient for the general good of the colony." How lofty! How true! Undoubtedly, these were the grandest words of government with the largest promise of any at that time uttered.

If more were needed to illustrate the new

可以回忆尊敬的牧师约翰·鲁宾逊的临别赠言，那是他为那些即将从代尔夫沙温出发去远航的清教徒们的致辞，这些话常常被引用，但永远不会过时。他的话多么甜美："如果上帝用他的神器向你们启示的话，那么请欣然接受，就如同你们通过我的布道欣然接受真理。但是我相信主会有更多启示和真理从他的圣言中迸发出来。"接下来这位优秀的牧师又公正地谴责了那些拒绝真理的人！"举个例子，路德的信徒无法超越路德的视野。无论上帝又进一步传给了卡尔文什么意旨，卡尔文的信徒们宁愿死去也不愿接受，于是他们就只能在原地踏步。这是一种令人惋惜的苦难，因为虽然这些人在当时是难得而耀眼的信徒，但是上帝并没有把所有的旨意向他们明示。"在这段话中，除了恰如其分的谴责，其中还有对人类进步规律的清楚的认识，而这在当时很少有人关注。不过正是这种认识指点了人类大家庭的稳步前进，也为世界展示了一个不断拓宽、永无尽头的未来前景。

那些清教徒的人数不多又很穷。这次历史性航行的全部装备，包括1700英镑的贸易股票，总计仅仅2400英镑。他们的要求甚少。当过兵的迈尔斯·斯坦迪什上尉被派往英格兰寻求帮助——不是军事上而是财力上的帮助（太不可思议

epoch, it would be found in the parting words of the venerable pastor, John Robinson, addrest to the Pilgrims, as they were about to sail from Delfshaven—words often quoted, yet never enough. How sweetly and beautifully he says: "And if God should reveal anything to you by any other instrument of his, be as ready to receive it as ever you were to receive any truth by my ministry; but I am confident that the Lord hath more light and truth yet to break forth out of his holy word." And then how justly the good preacher rebukes those who close their souls to truth! "The Lutherans, for example, can not be drawn to go beyond what Luther saw, and whatever part of God's will he hath further imparted to Calvin, they will rather die than embrace, and so the Calvinists stick where he left them. This is a misery much to be lamented, for tho they were precious, shining lights in their times, God hath not revealed his whole will to them." Beyond the merited rebuke, here is a plain recognition of the law of human progress little discerned at the time, which teaches the sure advance of the human family, and opens the vista of the ever-broadening, never-ending future on earth.

Our Pilgrims were few and poor. The whole outfit of this historic voyage, including £1,700 of trading stock, was only £2,400, and how little was required for their succor appears in the experience of the soldier Captain Miles Standish, who, being sent to England for assistance—not military, but financial—(God save the mark!) succeeded in

了！），他最终成功地借到了钱。你猜多少？——150 英镑。当然还有一些妨碍他们得到帮助的东西，历史学家补充道："50%的借款利息。"这位为借钱而漂洋过海的勇士借到的就这么多。后来一位使者是阿勒顿，他为殖民地借来 200 英镑，利息降到了 30%。显然，我们现今社会的放高利贷者同那些伦敦商人颇有渊源。但是我不知道当新英格兰的子孙被过高的利息压迫时，想到自己的祖先也曾如此，会不会感到一丝欣慰。

当初这一小群人前途暗淡、无依无靠、势单力薄，囊中羞涩，在骄傲和伟大的人眼中都是无名之辈，在当代历史上也是名不见经传；他们离开欧洲时，可谓身无长物。可是如今，他们却成了世界上最具光彩的人物。而五月花号也比希腊神话中的阿尔戈号船或者任何一个常胜将军的雄伟战舰都更为不朽。这在那个年代是难以预知的，而在今人眼中这一切的过程却历历在目。经得起时间考验和沧桑变化的伟大成就源自人类的灵魂。历代君主和内阁，陆军和海军的将军们，连同华丽的宫廷以及硝烟弥漫的战场，随着时间的流逝都已经不见踪影；但是那些贫穷卑微的真理的先驱，特别是那些提升人性和倡导人权的典范，以及维护民有、民权、民享的政体却永远不会从世界上消失，这样的先驱将永远不会被忘却，他们的名望将同他们

borrowing—how much do you suppose?—£150 sterling. Something in the way of help; and the historian adds, "tho at fifty per cent. interest." So much for a valiant soldier on a financial expedition. A later agent, Allerton, was able to borrow for the colony £200 at a reduced interest of thirty per cent. Plainly, the money-sharks of our day may trace an undoubted pedigree to these London merchants. But I know not if any son of New England, opprest by exorbitant interest, will be consoled by the thought that the Pilgrims paid the same.

And yet this small people—so obscure and outcast in condition—so slender in numbers and in means—so entirely unknown to the proud and great—so absolutely without name in contemporary records—whose departure from the Old World took little more than the breath of their bodies—are now illustrious beyond the lot of men; and the *Mayflower* is immortal beyond the Grecian *Argo*, or the stately ship of any victorious admiral. Tho this was little foreseen in their day, it is plain now how it has come to pass. The highest greatness surviving time and storm is that which proceeds from the soul of man. Monarchs and cabinets, generals and admirals, with the pomp of courts and the circumstance of war, in the gradual lapse of time disappear from sight; but the pioneers of truth, tho poor and lowly, especially those whose example elevates human nature and teaches the rights of man, so that government of the people, by the people, and for the people shall not perish

所为之奋斗的事业共存。

今天我有幸向你们致辞，但我不知道在座的各位中有谁想到了去回忆一下当五月花号开始其冒险之旅时，当时世界瞩目的那些权高位重的大人物的名字。愚蠢的詹姆士还坐在英国王位上，为“严惩了清教徒”而感到光荣。怪癖的路易斯八世，即黎塞留的傀儡，是当时的法国国王。低能的菲利普三世统治着西班牙和西印度群岛。迫害狂斐迪南二世，残酷地折磨新教徒，是德国国王。保罗五世，出自鲍格才家族，是罗马教皇。在当时的王侯之列中，还有丹麦国王克里斯蒂安四世和他的儿子——挪威亲王克里斯蒂安；瑞典国王古斯塔夫斯·阿道夫斯；波兰国王西格蒙德三世；波希米亚国王腓特烈，而他的妻子则是英国郁郁寡欢的伊丽莎白，是汉诺威王室的祖先；乔治·威廉是勃兰登堡的侯爵，也是普鲁士王室的祖先，而普鲁士王室后来出过一位德意志帝国的君主；马克西米连是巴伐利亚的公爵，而莫里斯是黑森的伯爵领主；克里斯蒂安是不伦瑞克和吕嫩堡的公爵；约翰·腓特烈是符腾堡和泰克的公爵；约翰，拿骚的伯爵；亨利，洛林的公爵；伊莎贝拉是西班牙公主，低地国家的君主；莫里斯是奥兰治王室的第四位王子；查尔斯·伊曼纽尔，萨瓦的公爵，是意大利联合王国国王的祖先；科斯莫·德·美第奇是弗罗伦

from the earth, such harbingers can never be forgotten, and their renown spreads co-extensive with the cause they served.

I know not if any whom I now have the honor of addressing have thought to recall the great in rank and power filling the gaze of the world as the *Mayflower* with her company fared forth on their adventurous voyage. The foolish James was yet on the English throne, glorying that he had "peppered the Puritans." The morose Louis XIII, through whom Richelieu ruled, was King of France. The imbecile Philip III swayed Spain and the Indies. The persecuting Ferdinand the Second, tormentor of Protestants, was Emperor of Germany. Paul V, of the House of Borghese, was Pope of Rome. In the same princely company and all contemporaries were Christian IV, King of Denmark, and his son Christian, Prince of Norway; Gustavus Adolphus, King of Sweden; Sigmund the Third, King of Poland; Frederick, King of Bohemia, with his wife, the unhappy Elizabeth of England, progenitor of the House of Hanover; George William, Margrave of Brandenburg, and ancestor of the Prussian house that has given an emperor to Germany; Maximilian, Duke of Bavaria; Maurice, landgrave of Hesse; Christian, Duke of Brunswick and Lunenburg; John Frederick, Duke of Würtemberg and Teck; John, Count of Nassau; Henry, Duke of Lorraine; Isabella, In fanta of Spain and ruler of the Low Countries; Maurice, fourth Prince of Orange; Charles Emanuel, Duke of Savoy and ancestor of the King of United Italy;

萨的第三位大公；安东尼奥·赖利是威尼斯的第93任总督，在其上任前发生了可怕的悲剧，也就是英国舞台上曾上演的“保存下来的威尼斯”；伯利恒·加博尔是集权的特兰西瓦尼亚的王子，他长着非洲人的面孔，被选为匈牙利国王；还有君士坦丁堡的苏丹王穆斯塔法是土耳其的第二十任统治者。

这些人在当时统治着欧洲，提起他们的名字常常令人敬畏，他们的容貌通过美术作品流传下来，所以今天对于好奇者来说他们的面目是可以看到的，就好像他们曾在这儿的街道上走过。请注意以下对比：从没有过艺术家为我们的祖先画像，而他们的容貌也无人知晓；但是比之当时任何威震全球的权贵，他们留下的是圣洁的回忆。教皇、皇帝、国王、伊斯兰教的苏丹、大公、公爵、总督、侯爷、封爵和伯爵，和登陆普利茅斯海岸巨砾滩的卑微人群相比，他们又算得了什么？他们拥有的其实只是世俗权力的标志，而我们的祖先拥有的是最宝贵的与生俱来的美德，他们的登陆是一个新纪元的开端。

在这些威武庄严的王公贵族中，现在又有哪位即便尚被人记起，却不会遭遇冷漠和鄙视呢？如果把古斯塔夫斯·阿道弗斯排除，那是因为他展现了优秀的品格。把五月花号和清教徒与称霸世界的君主们相比，前者正在升入天空而永久地闪耀

Cosmo dé Medici, third Grand Duke of Florence; Antonio Priuli, ninety-third Doge of Venice, just after the terrible tragedy commemorated on the English stage as "Venice Preserved"; Bethlehem Gabor, Prince of Unitarian Transylvania, and elected King of Hungary, with the countenance of an African; and the Sultan Mustapha, of Constantinople, twentieth ruler of the Turks.

Such at that time were the crowned sovereigns of Europe, whose names were mentioned always with awe, and whose countenances are handed down by art, so that at this day they are visible to the curious as if they walked these streets. Mark now the contrast. There was no artist for our forefathers, nor are their countenances now known to men; but more than any powerful contemporaries at whose tread the earth trembled is their memory sacred. Pope, emperor, king, sultan, grand-duke, duke, doge, margrave, landgrave, count—what are they all by the side of the humble company that landed on Plymouth Rock? Theirs indeed, were the ensigns of worldly power, but our Pilgrims had in themselves that inborn virtue which was more than all else besides, and their landing was an epoch.

Who in the imposing troop of worldly grandeur is now remembered but with indifference or contempt? If I except Gustavus Adolphus, it is because he revealed a superior character. Confront the *Mayflower* and the Pilgrims with the potentates who occupied such space in the world. The former are ascending into the firmament, there to

光芒,后者却一直在坠入被遗忘的黑谷,只有在指出某种教训或者说明他们所忽视的当年某些同代人的声望时才会被提及。如果我说这是最优秀品质的例证,是道德本质的胜利,我有错吗?起初也许困难重重,关山迢递,但他们最终取得了胜利。他们掌握着光明,只要冲破云层,就会放射出越来越灿烂的光彩。我经常会想,我若是一个牧师,有幸站在讲道台前,心中充满好友的热情鼓励,那么我就要从《圣经》中选这么一句话作为我的布道:"一点点酵母能发松整个面团。"除了我们清教徒的影响,我找不出更好的例子来解释这句话了。这一小群人,用自我牺牲、公正平等的法律、民主政府和对原则永远忠诚的榜样,正在将整个大陆发酵起来,并在适当的时候必会让整个世界发酵。通过他们的示范,共和制度得以推广,我们还将像他们那样去保障这些制度。

我们苦苦追求的自由,并不是单生的植物,公正常常伴之左右。但公正只能是应用于人类事务中的权利。请不要忘记,只有最高尚的品德才有最多的自由。一位伟大的诗人在他一首绝妙的十四行诗中谈到自己宝贵的财富时曾说:"爱宝之人首先必须聪明、善良。"因此清教徒用美好的典范,教

shine forever, while the latter have been long dropping into the darkness of oblivion, to be brought forth only to point a moral or illustrate the fame of contemporaries whom they regarded not. Do I err in supposing this an illustration of the supremacy which belongs to the triumphs of the moral nature? At first impeded or postponed, they at last prevail. Theirs is a brightness which, breaking through all clouds, will shine forth with ever-increasing splendor. I have often thought that if I were a preacher, if I had the honor to occupy the pulpit so grandly filled by my friend near me, one of my sermons should be from the text, "A little leaven shall leaven the whole lump." Nor do I know a better illustration of these words than the influence exerted by our Pilgrims. That small band, with the lesson of self-sacrifice, of just and equal laws, of the government of a majority, of unshrinking loyalty to principle, is now leavening this whole continent, and in the fulness of time will leaven the world. By their example, republican institutions have been commended, and in proportion as we imitate them will these institutions be assured.

Liberty, which we so much covet, is not a solitary plant. Always by its side is justice. But Justice is nothing but right applied to human affairs. Do not forget, I entreat you, that with the highest morality is the highest liberty. A great poet, in one of his inspired sonnets, speaking of his priceless possession, has said, "But who loves that must first be wise and good." Therefore do

我们去追求自由和共和制度，就像在古时候，苏格拉底和柏拉图在讲授智慧的课程时教人们去追求自由并且倡导共和那样。如果共和政体在任何地方失败了（比如说在某个讲西班牙语的美洲国家），那是因为他们缺少这些教诲，因为没有清教徒教给他们道德法则。

总统先生，我的这些想法表达得并不完善，我要感谢新英格兰祖先们赐予的恩惠，并且献上我的感恩之心。我不仅是在感恩节这天才会想起纪念他们。如果我能做到的话，我要让他们的榜样在全世界发扬光大，将他们的精神铭刻在大地上。那指引他们行动的良知应该成为我们公共委员会的指南。我们应该制定他们所坚持的公正平等的法律，继承他们坚持真理的热忱。我不会忘记他们的勇气和坚定。假如当时他们返航或者动摇了，我无法想象这片大陆的历史将会怎样，但我真切地知道我们将失去一个伟大的典范。要是哥伦布屈从于那些叛变的水手，并返回西班牙而没有实现伟大的发现，要是华盛顿因英国的强大以及新泽西的大雪而灰心地退缩了，我们就会缺少了这些给人们以勇气的伟大范例。我们的清教徒也是同样的英雄，他们的典范同样珍贵。

Pilgrims in their beautiful example teach liberty, teach republican institutions, as at an earlier day, Socrates and Plato, in their lessons of wisdom, taught liberty and helped the idea of the republic. If republican government has thus far failed in any experiment, as, perhaps, somewhere in Spanish America, it is because these lessons have been wanting. There have been no Pilgrims to teach the moral law.

Mr. President, with these thoughts, which I imperfectly express, I confess my obligations to the forefathers of New England, and offer to them the homage of a grateful heart. But not in thanksgiving only would I celebrate their memory. I would if I could make their example a universal lesson, and stamp it upon the land. The conscience which directed them should be the guide for our public councils. The just and equal laws which they required should be ordained by us, and the hospitality to truth which was their rule should be ours. Nor would I forget their courage and stedfastness. Had they turned back or wavered, I know not what would have been the record of this continent, but I see clearly that a great example would have been lost. Had Columbus yielded to his mutinous crew and returned to Spain without his great discovery; had Washington shrunk away disheartened by British power and the snows of New Jersey, these great instances would have been wanting for the encouragement of men. But our Pilgrims belong to the same heroic company, and their example is not less precious.

清教徒登陆普利茅斯海岸巨砾滩后不久，伟大的共和国诗人约翰·弥尔顿写下了追求美和真理的美妙剧本《科摩斯》。他的天性比清教徒更加文雅，但我们无需太多的想象就能理解剧中人物的台词，至少是那位受爱戴的牧师在终场时高雅而近乎天籁的语句：

追随我的人们爱的是道德天使，
只有她才是自由的化身。
她能让你的心灵升华，
超越教堂的钟声飞向天际彩云。
倘若道德天使法力不足，
天堂也会为她屈尊。

Only a short time after the landing on Plymouth Rock, the great republican poet, John Milton, wrote his "Comus," so wonderful for beauty and truth. His nature was more refined than that of the Pilgrims, and yet it requires little effort of imagination to catch from one of them, or at least from their beloved pastor, the exquisite, almost angelic words at the close:

Mortals, who would follow me,
Love Virtue; she alone is free;
She can teach ye how to climb
Higher than the sphery chime.
Or if Virtue feeble were,
Heaven itself would stoop to her.

7.

讲英语的民族

乔治·威廉·柯蒂斯[①]

尊敬的商会主席,各位先生们:

我心怀不安地答谢敬酒,因为我们受到了确凿的指责。虽然当今晚听到讲英语的民族说话太多的说法后,我们不相信会有人这么说,但这种说法确实存在。我们口才流利的英格兰大臣最近在诺丁汉机械学院祝贺他们废除了辩论俱乐部,并说他欣喜地憧憬着在各大院校都会设置“沉默”专业教授职位。我承认这个倡议此刻对我来说实在是太及时太明智了。要是我已经拿到了沉默学

①1824~1892,美国作家,公众演说家。

7.

The English–Speaking Race

By George William Curtis

Mr. Chairman and Gentlemen of the Chamber of Commerce:

I rise with some trepidation to respond to this toast, because we have been assured upon high authority, altho after what we have heard this evening we can not believe it, that the English–speaking race speaks altogether too much. Our eloquent Minister in England recently congratulated the Mechanics′ Institute at Nottingham that it had abolished its debating club, and said that he gladly anticipated the establishment in all great institutions of education of a professorship of Silence. I confess that the proposal never seemed to me so timely and wise as at this moment. If I had only taken a

的高等学位，主席先生，您该多么热情地来恭喜我，来庆贺这次快乐的聚会啊！

当费尔普斯先生进而说到美国人被禁止总是喋喋不休而且我们的演说家都是四年才能向公众唠叨一次时，我实在是太佩服他无限的想象力了。但是当他说到这种四年一度的释放让百姓感激这种演讲没有更频繁地出现时，我想他这种说法需要认真对待，必需让他去找迪普博士辩论一番。我相信，至少当我们尊贵的英国朋友们回到故土之后，定会急忙去找部长阁下，围着他打听四年才演讲一次的美国人都在哪里。只要他们留在这儿过冬，就会发现如果说美国人每四年才对公众演讲一次的话，那么他们却无时无刻不在私下里口若悬河。如果我们贵宾的经历与观察和我的一样幸运的话，那么他们必将发现两个英语民族都有不少演讲家——此刻离我不到一百英里远就有——就算他们每四个小时演讲一次，公众也愿意洗耳恭听。

温德尔·菲利普斯曾说过，一个美国婴儿刚刚可以在摇篮里坐起来时，他就给托儿所的人开会，并且进而对那些人大发议论。如果这种议员天分无法压抑，如果整年我们都一直在听演说、演讲、

high degree in silence, Mr. Chairman, how cordially you would congratulate me and this cheerful company!

When Mr. Phelps proceeded to say that Americans are not allowed to talk all the time, and that our orators are turned loose upon the public only once in four years, I was lost in admiration of the boundless sweep of his imagination. But when he said that the result of this quadrennial outburst was to make the country grateful that it did not come oftener, I saw that his case required heroic treatment, and must be turned over to Dr. Depew. I am sure, at least, that when our distinguished friends from England return to their native land they will hasten to besiege His Excellency to tell them where the Americans are kept who speak only once in four years. And if they will but remain through the winter, they will discover that if our orators are turned loose upon the public only once in four years, they are turned loose in private all the rest of the time; and if the experience and observation of our guests are as fortunate as mine, they will learn that there are certain orators of both branches of the English-speaking race——not one hundred miles from me at this moment——whom the public would gladly hear, if they were turned loose upon it every four hours.

Wendell Phillips used to say that as soon as a Yankee baby could sit up in his cradle, he called the nursery to order and proceeded to address the house. If this Parliamentary instinct is irrepressible,

讲座、布道，以及不停的新闻报道（虽然并非总是中听）——据说市长阁下是对新闻报道很关注的听众，那么我们至少可以感到欣慰，因为我们晓得一个爱说话的国度是一个自由的国度，讲英语的民族是不可战胜的自由之师。

主席先生，刚刚您已经看过的祝词，十分简明而全面描述了英语民族的历史特点。这个民族是共和政体的创始人，让我们在西方大陆上创造帝国的奇迹得到了验证——仅仅凭着步枪和斧头、犁和梭、茶壶和《圣经》、摇椅和识字课本、浴盆以及一部象征自由的宪法，这个民族从沿海地区出发越过阿勒格尼山脉，挺进大草原，直到再也听不见大西洋波涛的拍岸声、只闻太平洋的浪花在窃窃私语；宛如古代神话的美妙女神降临大地，鲜花与水果纷纷响应她的脚步声，在这个前进的民族长长的足迹后面，留下的是一个又一个快乐的州，涌现出一代比以前任何时候都更有智慧和富足的人们，而胜利进军的每一座更遥远的营地都是说英语民族的更前方的文明前哨。

这个民族是进步的先驱，在全世界甚至在海上最遥远的岛屿，这一点都被记录在公民、宗教和贸易自由的一页页历史上。每座机器哼唱的工厂，

if all the year round we are listening to orations, speeches, lectures, sermons, and the incessant, if not always soothing, oratory of the press, to which His Honor the Mayor is understood to be a closely attentive listener, we have at least the consolation of knowing that the talking countries are the free countries, and that the English-speaking races are the invincible legions of liberty.

The sentiment which you have read, Mr. Chairman, describes in a few comprehensive words the historic characteristics of the English-speaking race. That it is the founder of commonwealths, let the miracle of empire which we have wrought upon the Western Continent attest:—its advance from the seaboard with the rifle and the ax, the plow and the shuttle, the teapot and the Bible, the rocking-chair and the spelling-book, the bath-tub and a free constitution, sweeping across the Alleghanies, over-spreading the prairies and pushing on until the dash of the Atlantic in their ears dies in the murmur of the Pacific; and as the wonderful Goddess of the old mythology touched earth, flowers and fruits answered her footfall, so in the long trail of this advancing race, it has left clusters of happy States, teeming with a population, man by man, more intelligent and prosperous than ever before the sun shone upon, and each remoter camp of that triumphal march is but a further outpost of English-speaking civilization.

That it is the pioneer of progress, is written all over the globe to the utmost islands of the sea, and upon every page of the history of civil and

每一条铁路和每一列蒸汽火车，每一部电报机和电话机，改进了的农业体制，不断涌现的神奇发明，所有这些在很大程度上都是这个民族天才的表现。瓦特发明蒸汽机，带来动力能源；富兰克林发明避雷针，为人们带来安全；摩尔斯发明了电报，创造了神话。这个从国王手中夺取了政权的民族已经大获全胜，他们从王侯手中获得了最高统治的秘密，从天空、大地、河海那里获得了有益于进步的无限使用权。

这个民族是自由的坚强保卫者，这一点与我们的历史相符，因为美国的出现就是在英国殖民地上捍卫英国式的自由的结果，这些捍卫者有着英国血统，他们仍然自豪地讲着英语，珍惜着英国传统，珍惜着权利的平等，还像珍惜自己的光荣那样珍惜着英国的古老荣耀。

任何讲英语的人，即使他们愿意，也无法丢弃这个民族与众不同的名字，自从古希腊和朱迪亚那久远的时代，其名望的价值和荣耀无人可比。我们美国人也许曾嘲笑过英国上万次，我们也许有理由反对她，我们也许认为她的观点错误、政策愚蠢，但是除了英国，即便最具美国特征美国人还能从哪个国家得到推动美国进步和文明的独特动力呢？除了莎士比亚，汉普登，清教徒以及詹姆士国

religious and commercial freedom. Every factory that hums with marvelous machinery, every railway and steamer, every telegraph and telephone, the changed systems of agriculture, the endless and universal throb and heat of magical invention, are, in their larger part, but the expression of the genius of the race that with Watts drew from the airiest vapor the mightiest of motive powers, with Franklin leashed the lightning, and with Morse outfabled fairy lore. The race that extorted from kings the charter of its political rights has won, from the princes and powers of the air, the earth and the water, the secret of supreme dominion, the illimitable franchise of beneficent progress.

That it is the stubborn defender of liberty, let our own annals answer, for America sprang from the defense of English liberty in English colonies, by men of English blood, who still proudly speak the English language, cherish English traditions, and share of right, and as their own, the ancient glory of England.

No English-speaking people could, if it would, escape its distinctive name, and, since Greece and Judea, no name has the same worth and honor among men. We Americans may flout England a hundred times. We may oppose her opinions with reason, we may think her views unsound, her policy unwise; but from what country would the most American of Americans prefer to have derived the characteristic impulse of American development and civilization rather than England? What language would we rather speak

王的英语，我们宁愿讲什么语言呢？除了我们暗自夸赞的英国的快艇，我们宁愿选择什么快艇作为我们远航的工具呢？我们的国民生活、行为与思维方式、对品格与成就的评价标准，难道这些不是跟在英国下议院、英国会计室、英国车间和英国家庭中的那些如出一辙吗？

毫无疑问，原始的根株在新的分枝这儿有了本质上的变化。当美国人的目光穿越大海，望向霍桑高兴地称之为“我们的老家”的地方并且打量自己时，常会喃喃自语：“果肉出自水果，快意出自活力。”他留给英国的是一个反传统的清教徒形象，在宗教和国务问题上他成长为章程的改革者，他来到这儿的时候只是一把粗糙的铁棒而现在已经变成一柄利剑。他用铁一般的手腕征服了一个大陆，却用天鹅绒般的温柔来管理和教化它。对他来说，学校的铃声比任何音乐都悦耳；人人平等的原则在他心中比其他任何原则都宝贵；人人都将享有平等权利的希望比任何其他的憧憬都更迷人。

这就是美国佬，这就是那个新的分支，但是它的质地并不低劣或脆弱，而是成功地经历了千年风雨仍然坚韧的古老英国橡树的新枝。无论是老枝还是新枝让自由更上了一层楼，那都是高尚的

than the tongue of Shakespeare and Hampden, of the Pilgrims and King James´s version? What yachts, as a tribute to ourselves upon their own element, would we rather outsail than English yachts? In what national life, modes of thought, standards and estimates of character and achievement do we find our own so perfectly reflected as in the English House of Commons, in English counting-rooms and workshops, and in English homes?

No doubt the original stock has been essentially modified in the younger branch. The American, as he looks across the sea, to what Hawthorne happily called "Our old home," and contemplates himself, is disposed to murmur: "Out of the eater shall come forth meat and out of the strength shall come forth sweetness." He left England a Puritan iconoclast; he has developed in Church and State into a constitutional reformer. He came hither a knotted club; he has been transformed into a Damascus blade. He seized and tamed a continent with a hand of iron; he civilizes and controls it with a touch of velvet. No music is so sweet to his ear as the sound of the common-school bell; no principle so dear to his heart as the equal rights of all men; no vision so entrancing to his hope as those rights universally secured.

This is the Yankee; this is the younger branch; but a branch of no base or brittle fiber, but of the tough old English oak, which has weathered triumphantly the tempest of a thousand years. It is a noble contention whether the younger

竞争。但毫无疑问，大西洋两岸的共识是，自由是英国的传统。在英格兰民族特有的框架下，我们继承了它、拥有了它、传播了它。正如张伯伦先生所言那是法制下的自由。自由而非放纵；是文明而非野蛮；是穿着法律的神圣外衣的自由，因为只有法律才是人民意愿、代议政体、陪审团审判、人身保护、言论和出版自由的唯一权威体现——呃，主席先生，它们是我们的传家宝，是世代相传的钻石。在这大千世界上，它们和家族姓名，语言与传统，携手相伴。

先生，我代表在座的各方人士，也代表我个人，真心诚意地响应您祝词中的热切期盼："祝愿我们这个大家族的所有成员永远共同努力为世界造福。"其成员若是离心离德，那肯定将是世界的不幸。英美之间曾有过激烈和愤怒的争吵也是不可否认的。这个国家的党派精神对旧有的仇恨耿耿于怀时，无论它反对什么总是要打上英国名字的烙印。与英国的每一种分歧、每一次误解都被党派可耻地利用了。但是这来自同一民族的两个伟大分支已经成熟，每当遇到急需调停的严重问题时，他们都会把蛊惑人心的政客抛在一边，回想起

or the elder branch has further advanced the frontiers of liberty, but it is unquestionable that liberty, as we understand it on both sides of the sea, is an English tradition; we inherit it, we possess it, we transmit it, under forms peculiar to the English race. It is as Mr. Chamberlain has said, liberty under law. It is liberty, not license; civilization, not barbarism; it is liberty clad in the celestial robe of law, because law is the only authoritative expression of the will of the people, representative government, trial by jury, habeas corpus, freedom of speech and of the press—why, Mr. Chairman, they are the family heirlooms, the family diamonds, and they go wherever in the wide world go the family name and language and tradition.

Sir, with all my heart, and, I am sure, with the hearty assent of this great and representative company, I respond to the final aspiration of your toast: "May this great family in all its branches ever work together for the world's welfare." Certainly its division and alienation would be the world's misfortune. That England and America have had sharp and angry quarrels is undeniable. Party spirit in this country, recalling old animosity, has always stigmatized with the English name whatever it opposed. Every difference, every misunderstanding with England has been ignobly turned to party account; but the two great branches of this common race have come of age, and wherever they may encounter a serious difficulty which must be accommodated they have but to thrust

林肯总统那崇高的话语:“对人无恶意,广结善缘。”有了这种精神,有我身边各位先生所代表的精神和情感,我可以不揣冒昧地代你们对张伯伦先生说,没有任何误解不能被体面而愉快地解决。因为,来自两国的先生们,我们的民族有义务不仅去捍卫而且去示范宪法所赋予的自由。

问题并不是一个世纪前或本世纪初在先辈光辉的照耀下我们做了些什么,而是在这个国家的共和体制下和英国的议会体制下,按照民众政体的原则,我们今天的责任是什么。

只有大众的良知和大众的智慧能够保障我们不陷入人为冲突,我们民族的子孙才有理由享受自由,英语民族的繁荣才不会衰退。我相信前途光明。我相信光明正在不断增长,相信沉睡在一个同源民族身上的巨大力量将被激发出来,不是将两国分隔得更远,而是把两国更牢固地凝聚在一起共同捍卫法律保障下的自由。

demagogues aside, to recall the sublime words of Abraham Lincoln, "With malice toward none, with charity for all," and in that spirit, and in the spirit and the emotion represented in this country by the gentlemen upon my right and my left, I make bold to say to Mr. Chamberlain, in your name, there can be no misunderstanding which may not be honorably and happily adjusted. For to our race, gentlemen of both countries, is committed not only the defense, but the illustration of constitutional liberty.

The question is not what we did a century ago, or in the beginning of this century, with the lights that shone around us, but what is our duty today, in the light which is given to us of popular government under the republican form in this country, and the parliamentary form in England.

If a sensitive public conscience, if general intelligence should not fail to secure us from unnatural conflict, then liberty will not be justified of her children, and the glory of the English-speaking race will decline. I do not believe it. I believe that it is constantly increasing, and that the colossal power which slumbers in the arms of a kindred people will henceforth be invoked, not to drive them further asunder, but to weld them more indissolubly together in the defense of liberty under law.

8.

女人

霍勒斯·波特[1]

尊敬的总统和各位先生：

当大家为我举杯祝酒时，我坚持认为回敬祝酒的应该是一位讨女人欢心的单身男士。不过，在以女性所有制占主流的今天，已婚男人绝对是比任何人都更有女人缘的男人，而且据认为在这种情境下只有敢于向女士求爱的人才敢于向新英格兰协会发表演讲。

我知道今晚的这次祝酒并没有按照以往的顺序进行。按照惯例此次祝酒应该排在宴会的最后。这似乎是祝酒委员会做出的善意安排，给男人在

①1837 ~ 1921，美国外交官，军官。

8.

Woman

By Horace Porter

Mr. President and Gentlemen:

When this toast was proposed to me, I insisted that it ought to be responded to by a bachelor, by some one who is known as a ladies′ man; but in these days of female proprietorship it is supposed that a married person is more essentially a ladies′ man than anybody else, and it was thought that only one who had the courage to address a lady could have the courage, under these circumstances, to address the New England Society.

The toast, I see, is not in its usual order to-night. At public dinners this toast is habitually placed last on the list. It seems to be a benevolent provision of the Committee on Toasts in order to

一生中至少一次在回答女人时说了算的机会。不幸的是，在新英格兰的晚宴上，有关女人的讨论最富成果的话题与其说是女人的外貌不如说是女人的消失。据我所知这种情形已在几年前都市音乐厅举办一年一度的美食狂欢盛会时得以纠正。当时女士们被请到顶楼座位上从而为整个盛会增色不少。我深信这样的尝试是令人鼓舞的，因此有必要重复进行。当清教徒的后代们目光严肃地沉浸在清教徒的圣洁中时，那情景是多么美妙啊！看到那些虔诚的清教徒子孙哪怕只是一晚全心全意地把感情倾注到“上面提及之事”的时候，又是多么令人振奋呀！

女人的第一个家在伊甸园，在那儿男人第一次娶了女人。奇怪的是，这却让弥尔顿联想到了“失乐园”。上帝趁男人熟睡之时，将其一根肋骨抽出，用它造成女人，于是她便成了他的妻。恶毒的人总是告诉我们，男人的第一次睡眠因此便成了他最后一次休息。但如果女人偶尔会喜欢这种有时令我们无法理解的矛盾思想和邪恶心理，那么她一定要记住对她有利的一点，即她是从男人身上最弯曲的部分创造出来的。

关于人类的诞生犹太人有不同的理论。他们追溯到我们都是猴子的时代。他们坚持说男人最

give man in replying to Woman one chance at least in life of having the last word. At the New England dinners, unfortunately the most fruitful subject of remark regarding woman is not so much her appearance as her disappearance. I know that this was remedied a few years ago, when this grand annual gastronomic high carnival was held in the Metropolitan Concert Hall. There, ladies were introduced into the galleries to grace the scene by their presence; and I am sure the experiment was sufficiently encouraging to warrant repetition, for it was beautiful to see the descendants of the Pilgrims sitting with eyes upturned in true Puritanic sanctity it was encouraging to see the sons of those pious sires devoting themselves, at least for one night, to setting their affections upon "things above."

Woman's first home was in the Garden of Eden. There man first married woman. Strange that the incident should have suggested to Milton the "Paradise Lost." Man was placed in a profound sleep, a rib was taken from his side, a woman was created from it, and she became his wife. Evil-minded persons constantly tell us that thus man's first sleep became his last repose. But if woman be given at times to that contrariety of thought and perversity of mind which sometimes passeth our understanding, it must be recollected in her favor that she was created out of the crookedest part of man.

The Rabbins have a different theory regarding creation. They go back to the time when we were all monkeys. They insist that man was originally

早诞生的时候是长着尾巴的，在进化过程中，这种尾状附肢从男人身上分离开来被造成了女人。这似乎可以说明为什么女人习惯于发表一些拖泥带水好像“拖着尾巴”似的演讲了，而且给这一理论增色的是，即便在今天，丈夫们似乎还是习惯于走路时把太太们甩在身后。

第一个女人由于在伊甸园中除了自己的丈夫之外没发现有别的男人，甚至开始同魔鬼调情。如若伊甸园坐落在像爱尔兰一般安静祥和的土地上，人类可能会免去诸多灾难苦痛，在那儿至少不会有蛇进入伊甸园。女人对知识充满渴望，在对蛇的盘问中真正地显示了女性刨根问底的特性。为了纪念这一事件，蛇好像总是把身体弄成蜷曲状，这种形状在几乎所有语言中都被用作了疑问的符号。不久人类第一对父母的家庭战争便爆发了。第一个女人最心爱的儿子被木棍打死了，所以直到今天已婚女人仍然对俱乐部有着本能的畏惧（在英语中，木棍和俱乐部是同一英语单词 club——译者注）。第一个女人知道是该隐拿起木棍杀害了亚伯；而现代的女人则认为是俱乐部引起的事端。但今晚我认出了一些面孔，他们曾在某天下午在第五大道俱乐部的玻璃窗后面出现过，当女人从

created with a kind of Darwinian tail, and that in the process of evolution this caudal appendage was removed and created into woman. This might better account for those Caudle lectures which woman is in the habit of delivering, and some color is given to this theory, from the fact that husbands even down to the present day seem to inherit a general disposition to leave their wives behind.

The first woman, finding no other man in that garden except her own husband, took to flirting even with the Devil. The race might have been saved much tribulation if Eden had been located in some calm and tranquil land——like Ireland. There would at least have been no snakes there to get into the garden. Now woman in her thirst after knowledge, showed her true female inquisitiveness in her cross-examination of the serpent, and, in commemoration of that circumstance the serpent seems to have been curled up and used in nearly all languages as a sign of interrogation. Soon the domestic troubles of our first parents began. The first woman's favorite son was killed with a club, and married women even to this day seem to have an instinctive horror of clubs. The first woman learned that it was Cain that raised a club. The modern woman has learned that it is a club that raises cain. Yet, I think, I recognize faces here to-night that I see behind the windows of Fifth Avenue clubs of an afternoon, with their noses pressed flat against the broad plate glass, and as woman trips along the sidewalk, I

人行道上袅袅婷婷地走过时，我瞅见这些先生鼻子紧贴在宽大的玻璃上看得两眼发直，其如痴如醉的程度，远远超过政府科学委员会观测金星运行时的痴迷程度（金星的英文是 Venus，而 Venus 又是神话中爱与美的女神——译者注）。

从窗前经过的许多女人都有着比天后朱诺和美第奇的维纳斯还要标致的脸庞。其中有金发碧眼的撒克逊裔美人，她眉目传情勾人魂魄，她那柔软光滑的金色秀发如浓密的金羊毛一般披在肩头，一丝一缕都像是清晨金色的阳光；还有褐色头发的拉丁裔白人美女，她眼睛黑亮而深邃，漆黑的美睫如同丝质的流苏点缀在珍珠一样白净细腻的脸颊上，看上去恰似渡鸦在新落的白雪上展开的翅膀。

但是在俱乐部中的男人并不幸福。随着时代不断向前推进，女人在物质方面不断地提升自己的生存水准。现在她无所顾忌、心气儿越来越高。她要求男女同校教育，她把探索分析科学高级领域中最深奥的问题视作小菜一碟。不论是借助于旧的还是新的计算时间的方法，她们都能准确地推算出丈夫应该回家的时间。我只听说过一个已婚男人利用时间计算方法的变更在家里明显地占到了便宜。这个男人是他家隔壁俱乐部的常客，他妻子经常责怪他晚上回家太迟。幸运的是，人们在

have observed that these gentlemen appear to be more assiduously engaged than ever was a government scientific commission, in taking observations upon the transit of Venus.

Before those windows passes many a face fairer than that of the Ludovician Juno or the Venus of Medici. There is the Saxon blonde with the deep blue eye, whose glances return love for love, whose silken tresses rest upon her shoulders like a wealth of golden fleece, each thread of which looks like a ray of the morning sunbeam. There is the Latin brunette with the deep, black, piercing eye, whose jetty lashes rest like a silken fringe upon the pearly texture of her dainty cheek, looking like raven's wings spread out upon new-fallen snow.

And yet the club man is not happy. As the ages roll on woman has materially elevated herself in the scale of being. Now she stops at nothing. She soars. She demands the co-education of sexes. She thinks nothing of delving into the most abstruse problems of the higher branches of analytical science. She can cipher out the exact hour of the night when her husband ought to be home, either according to the old or the recently adopted method of calculating time. I never knew of but one married man who gained any decided domestic advantage by this change in our time. He was a habitué of a club situated next door to his house. His wife was always upbraiding him for coming home too late at night. Fortunately, when they made this change of time, they placed one of

变更时间计算方法时，一条计时的子午线恰被划定在俱乐部和他的住宅的正中间。这样一来，每当他跨过那条虚拟的直线时，他便提前了一个小时。他发现他可以凌晨一点从俱乐部离开而十二点回到妻子身边。二十年来他的家庭第一次有了安宁。

现在的女性甚至对数字天文学感到着迷。给一个女人十分钟的时间她就能描述出天空的日心视差；给她二十分钟她能利用月球极点测量出某地的经度。但是给一个女人一个半小时去研究流行服饰，她甚至找不到自己裙子上的口袋在何处。

但是男人对女人的爱慕从未停息。他会把一半财产给她，会把整颗心给她，除了自己马车上的位置，他似乎总是情愿把自己拥有的一切给她。

每一个国家都有男性英雄和巾帼英雄。在英国战争中就有一个弗洛伦斯·南丁格尔。士兵们为了表示对她的崇拜，在她经过时纷纷俯身亲吻其外衣上的褶边。在美国的战争中有一位玛丽·沃克医生。没有人俯身亲吻过她外衣的褶边，因为实际上她从不穿那种服装。既然女人有足够的能力为自己辩护，为什么男人还要试图充当她们的代言

those meridians from which our time is calculated right between the club and his house. Every time he stept across that imaginary line it set him back a whole hour in time. He found that he could then leave his club at one o'clock and get home to his wife at twelve; and for the first time in twenty years peace reigned around the hearthstone.

Woman now revels even in the more complicated problems of mathematical astronomy. Give a woman ten minutes and she will describe a heliocentric parallax of the heavens. Give her twenty minutes and she will find astronomically the longitude of a place by means of lunar culminations. Give that same woman an hour and a half with the present fashions, and she can not find the pocket in her dress.

And yet man's admiration for woman never flags. He will give her half his fortune; he will give her his whole heart; he seems always willing to give her everything that he possesses, except his seat in a horse-car.

Every nation has had its heroines as well as its heroes. England, in her wars, had a Florence Nightingale; and the soldiers in the expression of their adoration, used to stoop and kiss the hem of her garment as she passed. America, in her war, had a Dr. Mary Walker. Nobody ever stooped to kiss the hem of her garment—because that was not exactly the kind of a garment she wore. But why should man stand here and attempt to speak for woman, when she is so abundantly equipped to speak for herself. I know that is the case in New

人呢？据我了解，在新英格兰就有这种越俎代庖的现象。今晚在这里看到格兰特将军使我想起了一件事以证明我以上所说的话，这件事发生在战后格兰特将军在新英格兰旅行的时候。火车停在了缅因州的一个火车站，将军就站在最后一列车厢后面的空廊上。大家知道当时他还没有向新英格兰协会发表一系列的精彩演说，所以一向以沉默寡言而远近闻名。人们总是谈到他身上令新英格兰敬慕的品质——沉默克制，从不在他人面前说东道西。突然间人群中出现一阵骚动，当车门打开时，一个又高又大、面容憔悴的女人冲出来气喘吁吁地朝车厢跑去。她从头顶摘下眼镜架在鼻子上，双手叉腰，抬头说道："我跑了差不多两英里才赶到这儿，急急忙忙得就是想看一眼这个一直让女人当代言者的男人。"

今晚的首位正式发言人（威廉·埃瓦茨）也谈及了女人，但那只是顺便提及，只涉及到摩门教和犹他州那个不幸的地方，在那里一个男人的去世可能让十二个女人成为寡妇。

昨天，在布鲁克林的新英格兰宴会上，一位发言人（亨利·沃德·比彻）试图证明摩门教徒最初来自新罕布什尔州和佛蒙特。我知道新英格兰男

England; and I am reminded, by seeing General Grant here to–night, of an incident in proof of it which occurred when he was making that marvelous tour through New England, just after the war. The train stopt at a station in the State of Maine. The General was standing on the rear platform of the last car. At that time, as you know, he had a great reputation for silence—for it was before he had made his series of brilliant speeches before the New England Society. They spoke of his reticence—a quality which New Englanders admire so much—in others. Suddenly there was a commotion in the crowd, and as it opened a large, tall, gaunt–looking woman came rushing toward the car, out of breath. Taking her spectacles off from the top of her head and putting them on her nose, she put her arms akimbo, and looking up, said: "Well, I've just come down here a runnin' nigh onto two mile, right on the clean jump, just to get a look at the man that lets the women do all the talkin'."

The first regular speaker of the evening (William M. Evarts) touched upon woman, but only incidentally, only in reference to Mormonism and that sad land of Utah, where a single death may make a dozen widows.

A speaker at the New England dinner in Brooklyn last night (Henry Ward Beecher) tried to prove that the Mormons came originally from New Hampshire and Vermont. I know that a New Englander sometimes in the course of his life marries several times; but he takes the precaution

人一生中有时会结几次婚，但他会按照合法的程序依次娶妻。与摩门教徒的不同之处在于他们将妻子排成纵列驾驭，而摩门教徒则是将妻子并列驾驭。

然而总统先生，即使我们中间最不严肃的人在思考女人品质的真正高贵之处时也会变得严肃。如果她真的是由肋骨所造，那么她就是由离男人心脏最近的那一部分造成的。

有种美丽的传说——男人是用大地的灰尘所造，而女人则是上帝按照自己的形象所造。在这片土地上，值得我们骄傲的一点是女人的品德便是其最好的防御，女性的贞操不必由目光灼灼的护士检测；女人在这片土地上，无论是大路还是偏僻小路，在女性自己高尚德行的可靠庇护下，她会不受凌辱和骚扰地四处散步。甚至是在罪恶肆虐的大都市或西部荒僻的峡谷矿区，在女人崇高的付出和她们榜样的影响下，仍然会有品质高洁的女孩成为孝顺的女儿、忠贞的妻子以及尽责的母亲。她们在那样恶劣的环境中仍能洁身自好，就像是生长在池塘中的睡莲一样。虽然周围杂草丛生妄图羁绊她的成长，尽管周围满是臭气污秽想要破坏她的纯洁，她仍能出淤泥而不染，迎着阳光不卑不亢地抬起美丽的脸庞。

见证过美国女儿们在战场上的英勇表现的人

to take his wives in their proper order of legal succession. The difference is that he drives his team of wives tandem, while the Mormon insists upon driving his abreast.

But even the least serious of us, Mr. President, have some serious moments in which to contemplate the true nobility of woman's character. If she were created from a rib, she was made from that part which lies nearest a man's heart.

It has been beautifully said that man was fashioned out of the dust of the earth while woman was created from God's own image. It is our pride in this land that woman's honor is her own best defense; that here female virtue is not measured by the vigilance of detective nurses; that here woman may walk throughout the length and the breadth of this land, through its highways and byways, uninsulted, unmolested, clothed in the invulnerable panoply of her own woman's virtue; that even in places where crime lurks and vice prevails in the haunts of our great cities, and in the rude mining gulches of the West, owing to the noble efforts of our women, and the influence of their example, there are raised, even there, girls who are good daughters, loyal wives, and faithful mothers. They seem to rise in those rude surroundings as grows the pond lily, which is entangled by every species of rank growth, environed by poison, miasma and corruption, and yet which rises in the beauty of its purity and lifts its fair face unblushing to the sun.

No one who has witnessed the heroism of

都会给予她们高度的赞扬。在这儿我指的并不单单是那些训练有素的仁爱会修女，她们好像上帝派来的天使总是出现在世界上多灾多难的地方，我指的还有另外一些美丽的女孩子，她们来自新英格兰以及其他州的优越家庭，从没经历过苦难场合的磨难也不习惯在帐篷中的简陋生活，可是她们却把包括时间、健康乃至生命在内的自己的一切无怨无悔地奉献给了崇高的事业。这种奉献深深地感动了我们的民族。当其中的一个女孩体态优雅地从野战医院光线暗淡的走廊中静静走过时，当她的裙脚轻轻摆动带起的微风拂上伤员的脸庞时，他们感觉到了仁爱天使正在用翅膀轻轻地吹拂他们干裂的额头。

啊！总统先生，女人毕竟是神秘的！有句话说得好，女人是十九世纪的一大谜题。然而如果我们无法猜透她，我们也就将永远与她难分难弃！

America's daughters in the field should fail to pay a passing tribute to their worth. I do not speak alone of those trained Sisters of Charity, who in scenes of misery and woe seem Heaven's chosen messengers on earth; but I would speak also of those fair daughters who come forth from the comfortable firesides of New England and other States, little trained to scenes of suffering, little used to the rudeness of a life in camp, who gave their all, their time, their health, and even life itself as a willing sacrifice in that cause which then moved the nation's soul. As one of these, with her graceful form, was seen moving silently through the darkened aisles of an army hospital, as the motion of her passing dress wafted a breeze across the face of the wounded, they felt that their parched brows had been fanned by the wings of the angel of mercy.

Ah! Mr. President, woman is after all a mystery. It has been well said, that woman is the great conundrum of the nineteenth century; but if we can not guess her, we will never give her up.

9.

献给赫伯特·斯宾塞的赞辞

威廉·埃瓦茨[1]

先生们：

我们今晚来到这儿表达美国人民对我们贵宾的感情。由于没有哪一个房间或城市能够容得下他所有朋友和仰慕者，所以有必要以某种方式在大众中筛选出一群人，而今天包括妇女在内的现场嘉宾是经过自然筛选的，这是多么好的办法啊！基于人类理性的本能和经验，我们很难在宴会的末尾继续哲学和进化论等玄奥的重大话题，而正是这些话题构成了斯宾塞先生对于当代知识和智慧的贡献。

①1818~1901，曾任美国纽约州参议员，美国司法部长及美国国务卿。

9.

Tribute to Herbert Spencer

By William M. Evarts

Gentlemen:

We are here tonight, to show the feeling of Americans toward our distinguished guest. As no room and no city can hold all his friends and admirers, it was necessary that a company should be made up by some method out of the mass, and what so good a method as that of natural selection and the inclusion, within these walls, of the ladies? It is a little hard upon the rational instincts and experiences of man that we should take up the abstruse subjects of philosophy and of evolution, of all the great topics that make up Mr. Spencer's contribution to the learning and the wisdom of his time, at this end of the dinner.

有一种愚昧在最古老的国度，甚至在其最原始的状态下就发生过。当一个人想要从别人的思想中汲取灵感或是猜测别人思想时，都必须禁食。一个在很多方面都值得我们学习的民族曾有一句格言。这个格言从常识上看是大家可以接受的。他们说一个经常饱腹之人难以探索奥秘。现在，以我个人对在座诸位的了解，大家都是经常饱腹之人。在公众宴会上，我曾就所有话题、出于各种目的为他们发表演讲，他们来到这里有不同的需求，但无论他们曾产生过怎样的共鸣，都符合经常饱腹之躯的概念。在原始时期，人们就有一种习惯，那种习惯与我们在今天的餐桌上的做法很相似，即各取所需。如果人们渴望拥有某人的学识、智慧、思辨力、勇气、优点，那么当这个人死后人们就会立即将他分食。那时唯一的不同是，人们会根据他的胖瘦决定将其烧烤还是蒸煮。现在让我们摆脱局限，看一看我们是带着多么复杂的心情和世俗的影响来到这佳肴丰富、美酒杂陈的宴会的，看一看

The most ancient nations, even in their primitive condition, saw the folly of this, and when one wished either to be inspired with the thoughts of others or to be himself a diviner of the thoughts of others, fasting was necessary, and a people from whom I think a great many things might be learned for the good of the people of the present time, have a maxim that will commend itself to your common-sense. They say the continually stuffed body can not see secret things. Now, from my personal knowledge of the men I see at these tables, they are owners of continually stuffed bodies. I have addrest them at public dinners, on all topics and for all purposes, and whatever sympathy they may have shown with the divers occasions which brought them together, they come up to this notion of continually stuffed bodies. In primitive times they had a custom which we only under the system of differentiation practise now at this dinner. When men wished to possess themselves of the learning, the wisdom, the philosophy, the courage, the great traits of any person, they immediately proceeded to eat him up as soon as he was dead, having only this diversity in that early time that he should be either roasted or boiled according as he was fat or thin. Now out of that narrow compass, see how by the process of differentiation and of multiplication of effects we have come to a dinner of a dozen courses and wines of as many varieties; and that simple process of appropriating the virtue and the wisdom of the great man that was brought before

事先打算借用伟人美德与智慧的简单程序如何在众多演讲者巧妙操作下，变成了对所有在座者进行分析的过程。毫无疑问，跟保持所有风俗的特色是一种艺术一样，烧烤我们的朋友并把我们所恨的人放入开水中也常常被认为是一门伟大的艺术，至少被认为是一种极大的愉悦。

斯宾塞先生，今天我们很高兴在这儿与您幸会。我们很高兴见到您同时也很高兴让您见到我们。我们很高兴见到您因为我们了解您拥有对您的民族极有价值的渊博知识和任何其他人都无法展示给我们的深透的理解力。我们很高兴见到您，因为在我们看来您能运用敏锐的智慧和深刻的洞察力对丰富的知识进行分析和重组，而这种智慧和洞察力是他人即使在涉及自己专业知识的微小课题上都不具备的。我们认为您在神学、心理学、自然科学、对单独的人及其观点的认识和从社会固有的意义出发对世界的认识等领域中的探讨都超越了一般的知识界人士。而正是这些学识构成了值得了解、值得探讨、值得规划并值得为之奋斗的世界。在我们看来，您已经享有并将在未来继续享有和中世纪阿尔贝图斯·马格纳斯曾享有过的同样的盛誉。他是当时最博学的人，在神学、心理

the feast is now diversified into an analysis of all the men here under the cunning management of many speakers. No doubt, preserving as we do the identity of all these institutions it is often considered a great art, or at least a great delight, to roast our friends and put in hot water those against whom we have a grudge.

Now, Mr. Spencer, we are glad to meet you here. We are glad to see you and we are glad to have you see us. We are glad to see you, for we recognize in the breadth of your knowledge, such knowledge as is useful to your race, a greater comprehension than any living man has presented to our generation. We are glad to see you, because in our judgment you have brought to the analysis and distribution of this vast knowledge a more penetrating intelligence and a more thorough insight than any living man has brought even to the minor topics of his special knowledge. In theology, in psychology, in natural science, in the knowledge of individual man and his exposition and in the knowledge of the world in the proper sense of society, which makes up the world, the world worth knowing, the world worth speaking of, the world worth planning for, the world worth working for, we acknowledge your labors as surpassing those of any of our kind. You seem to us to carry away and maintain in the future the same measure of fame among others that we are told was given in the Middle Ages to Albertus Magnus, the most learned man of those times, whose comprehension of theology, of psychology,

学、博物学、政治、历史以及研究方法等方面的造诣无疑是前无古人的。但是人们发现他的知识不过是一种量的积累，他并没有在他获得的学识之上添加任何新的经验或新的内容。

我刚才说过我们很高兴让您见到我们。在欢迎会上我们已经分享了您独一无二的大作，我们也希望在您安全抵达大西洋彼岸的时候，能让世界更详尽、更彻底地了解我们的优点和缺点。将整个国家、整个时代置于解剖台上并找出其所有的动脉、静脉及生命的搏动是我们自己的任何一家医学院力所不能及的。您给予我们的对人类的认识实用而有价值。不论针对您的体系或跟您持相同观点的体系会有怎样的断言或争议，也不管别人如何将您的体系与以前可与之媲美的体系进行比较，我们都必须承认它是可行、仁爱、严肃、恭敬的体系；我们也必须承认它力图取得德行的最高成就、它将罪恶看作是短暂而不是永恒的存在；同时我们也必须承认它有望达成在太平盛世的协助下力求达到的目标，那是一种至高的道德境界和无上幸福的状态。如果我们能够通过这些进程和

of natural history, of politics, of history, and of learning, comprehended more than any man since the classic time certainly; and yet it was found of him that his knowledge was rather an accumulation, and that he had added no new processes and no new wealth to the learning which he had achieved.

Now, I have said that we are glad to have you see us. You have already treated us to a very unique piece of work in this reception, and we are expecting perhaps that the world may be instructed after you are safely on the other side of the Atlantic in a more intimate and thorough manner concerning our merits and our few faults. This faculty of laying on a dissecting board an entire nation or an entire age and finding out all the arteries and veins and pulsations of their life is an extension beyond any that our own medical schools afford. You give us that knowledge of man which is practical and useful, and whatever the claims or the debates may be about your system or the system of those who agree with you, and however it may be compared with other competing systems that have preceded it, we must all agree that it is practical, that it is benevolent, that it is serious and that it is reverent; that it aims at the highest results in virtue; that it treats evil, not as eternal, but as evanescent, and that it expects to arrive at what is sought through the aid of the millennium—that condition of affairs in which there is the highest morality and the greatest happiness. And if we can come to that by these

指示达到这种状态，那么对这个民族而言无论它被冠以科学道德、数学自由或是其他普通的名称都无关紧要。请大家斟满酒杯为我们的贵客赫伯特·斯宾塞的健康干杯！

processes and these instructions, it matters little to the race whether it be called scientific morality and mathematical freedom or by another less pretentious name. You will please fill your glasses while we propose the health of our guest, Herbert Spencer.

10.

帝国之州

昌西·迪普[①]

尊敬的总统和各位先生：

不知从何时起，每年回敬祝酒变成了我的职责。当我收到委员会的邀请时，其独出心裁之处令我惊讶而不知所措。然而委员会请我做演讲是有所考虑的。今年是总统选举年，这使人们都不愿让自己涉及危险的话题。纽约州却非常安全，自从颇有才干的现任州长就职后，新英格兰协会已经数次让我代其回敬祝酒。或许这是由于他这位新英

①1834~1928，毕业于耶鲁大学，著名演说家，曾任美国纽约州参议员。

10.

The Empire State

By Chauncey M. Depew

Mr. President and Gentlemen:

It has been my lot from a time whence I can not remember to respond each year to this toast. When I received the invitation from the committee, its originality and ingenuity astonished and overwhelmed me. But there is one thing the committee took into consideration when they invited me to this platform. This is a Presidential year, and it becomes men not to trust themselves talking on dangerous topics. The State of New York is eminently safe. Ever since the present able and distinguished Governor has held his place I have been called upon by the New England Society to respond for him. It is probably due to

格兰人特别喜欢制造争论。这位州长是民主党人，而我却是共和党人。凡是他所信仰的都是我所憎恶的；凡是他所欣赏的都是我所反感的。大家对这次祝酒的热烈反应使我相信他的管理工作得到了新英格兰协会的一致认可。如果我没有误解鲁宾逊州长的看法，那么他宁愿当选为首席法官的不是约翰·凯利先生；假如我正确领会了凯利先生当众的发言，那么他也希望纽约州的州长不是卢修斯·鲁宾逊。因此在一次十分激烈的争论后，我们一致将阿朗索·科内尔推选为州长。在一次霍勒斯·格里利作为州长候选人的州代表大会上，代表们并没有推举最适合这一职位的人任州长。在回去的路上，他对我说："眼前没人能够在短时间内说出纽约州前十位州长的名字，我不明白为什么还会有人想当纽约州州长。"虽然曾经有过各色各样的州长，然而当提到州长一职时，就不得不提到几百年前的一个人物——纽约州的荷兰籍州长，有一条木头假肢的彼得·斯特伊扶桑特。当然还有出色的女州长们，人们常为她们写下赞美诗篇并为她们慷慨陈词，但是没有人能与散发着无穷魅力的荷兰籍女州长安妮可·扬斯相媲美。

that element in the New Englander that he delights in provoking controversy. The Governor is a Democrat, and I am a Republican. Whatever he believes in I detest; whatever he admires I hate. The manner in which this toast is received leads me to believe that in the New England Society his administration is unanimously approved. Governor Robinson, if I understand correctly his views, would rather that any other man should have been elected as Chief Magistrate than Mr. John Kelly. Mr. Kelly, if I interpret aright his public utterances, would prefer any other man for the Governor of New York than Lucius Robinson, and therefore, in one of the most heated controversies we have ever had, we elected a Governor by unanimous consent or assent in Alonzo B. Cornell. Horace Greeley once said to me, as we were returning from a State convention where he had been a candidate, but the delegates had failed to nominate the fittest man for the place: "I don't see why any man wants to be Governor of the State of New York, for there is no one living who can name the last ten Governors on a moment's notice." But tho there have been Governors and Governors, there is, when the gubernatorial office is mentioned, one figure that strides down the centuries before all the rest; that is the old Dutch Governor of New York, with his wooden leg—Peter Stuyvesant. There have been heroines, too, who have aroused the poetry and eloquence of all times, but none who have about them the substantial aroma of the Dutch heroine, Anneke Jans.

所有活着的人都不会忘记《爱丁堡书评》曾对整个美国文学不屑一顾地嘲讽道："谁会读一本美国书？"但正是在美国的荒原上华盛顿·欧文开辟出了一条通往无数天才成名必经的大路。而后来又有许多人如朗费罗、惠蒂埃、霍桑、普雷斯科特等追随他的足迹，而且他们的作品风靡全世界，他们本人也将永远受到最高的赞誉。

在这个群星灿烂的共和国中，纽约州取得了辉煌的物质成就。这些成就提供了这个国家中最好的公益；不仅如此，她在政治体制上也成为整个国家命运的主宰者。美国跟着纽约走。她的声音表明下届总统将是有着新英格兰血统的人或是新英格兰思想的代言人。

下面我要为没有获选的先生讲一个新英格兰人的故事。一个葬礼正在伯希尔的山里举行，哀悼者被安排到一间小客厅中。其中有一个典型的新英格兰女性，她对死者充满同情的同时又带有些许好奇。她环视完昏暗的房间后，对刚刚失去丈夫的寡妇说道："你们什么时候买的那座八日大座钟？"那个女人答道："我们没买新的大座钟呀"。"没有吗？那墙角放的是什么？""哦，不，那不是大座钟，那是我去世的丈夫，我们把他立起来好给

It is within the memory of men now living when the whole of American literature was dismissed with the sneer of the *Edinburgh Review*, " Who reads an American book?" But out of the American wilderness a broad avenue to the highway which has been trod by the genius of all times in its march to fame was opened by Washington Irving, and in his footsteps have followed the men who are read of all the world, and who will receive the highest tributes in all times–Longfellow, and Whittier, and Hawthorne and Prescott.

New York is not only imperial in all those material results which constitute and form the greatest commonwealth in this constellation of commonwealths, but in our political system she has become the arbiter of our national destiny. As goes New York so goes the Union, and her voice indicates that the next President will be a man with New England blood in his veins or a representative of New England ideas.

And for the gentleman who will not be elected I have a Yankee story. In the Berkshire hills there was a funeral, and as they gathered in the little parlor there came the typical New England female, who mingles curiosity with her sympathy, and as she glanced around the darkened room she said to the bereaved widow, "When did you get that new eight–day clock?" "We ain't got no new eight–day clock," was the reply. "You ain't? What's that in the corner there?" "Why no, that's not an eight–day clock, that's the deceased;

哀悼者们腾出些地方。”

在大约五十年前新英格兰所有的公路都通往波士顿，但是在最近的五十年间，不论是偏僻小路还是公路每条都通往纽约。纽约成了新英格兰地区的首府。在这里的新英格兰人的人数比新英格兰州其他地方的新英格兰人的总数还要多三倍。今天在新英格兰的山坡上耕作、在学校里寄宿教书和将要成为未来商界王子或杰出律师或精明政治家的小伙子们，都把目光投向了纽约而不是波士顿，把纽约当成一个大有可为的地方。新英格兰的子孙们，我们对你们是多么地慷慨啊！我们将你们安排在最好的职位上、把你们培养成商界巨子。在这个州中哪个城市、哪个村庄里不是你们居住着最好的房舍、经营着最大的工厂、控制着最关键的行业？我们曾多次推选你们中的一员为州长，我们让你们处在你尊我荣的地位上。在政府内阁中有来自纽约州的杰出的国务卿，他的纯正新英格兰血统使他成为帝国之州最合适、最出色的代表。

尽管我们尽最大的努力去满足新英格兰人，但有一件事我们始终无法做到。我们能够满足他的雄心、填满他的钱包，却不能满足他的胃口。今

we stood him on end, to make room for the mourners."

Up to within fifty years ago all roads in New England led to Boston; but within the last fifty years every byway and highway in New England leads to New York. New York has become the capital of New England, and within her limits are more Yankees than in any three New England States combined. The boy who is today ploughing the stony hillside in New England, who is boarding around and teaching school, and who is to be the future merchant-prince or great lawyer, or wise statesman, looks not now to Boston, but to New York, as the El Dorado of his hopes. And how generously, sons of New England, have we treated you? We have put you in the best offices; we have made you our merchant-princes. Where is the city or village in our State where you do not own the best houses, run the largest manufactories, and control the principal industries? We have several times made one of your number Governor of the State, and we have placed you in positions where you honor us while we honor you. New York's choice in the National Cabinet is the distinguished Secretary of State, whose pure Yankee blood renders him none the less a most fit and most eminent representative of the Empire State.

But while we have done our best to satisfy the Yankee, there is one thing we have never been able to do. We can meet his ambition and fill his purse, but we never can satisfy his stomach.

晚总统曾说过普利茅斯海岸巨砾滩是在二十一日庆祝周年纪念日，而我们却是在二十二日。他没说真正的原因。不像他所说的只是日期上存在的分歧。事实上，普利茅斯海岸的猪肉和菜豆满足不了新英格兰人庞大的胃口，他们把纪念日选在二十一日是想在当晚乘火车以便在二十二日抵达纽约州，赶上一年一度的盛宴。从 1620 年到纽约州开始接纳移民定居，新英格兰人一直感到肚子里很空，即便是现在不论是土生土长的或是后来迁入的新英格兰人还是要找世界上最豪华的饭店以满足他们的口腹之需。于是他们便来到了这家店，在这座美国最大的饭店里他们或许每年都能获得一次满足感。

我的朋友柯蒂斯先生曾在他演讲的开头极富说服力地提到荷兰人对旧清教徒的看法；在演讲结束的时候他又提及现代人对清教徒的观点。清教徒虽然让人不堪忍受，但在二百多年前那却是一群出色的历史性人物。先生们，如果你们当中的任何一位被迫离开今晚的节日盛宴而回到两百多年前，与你们的祖先们同吃同住、听他们讲话，我的同胞们，那将是怎样的情景啊！尽管就能力而言清教徒都会有不少很好的机会，但在他们胜任所做的工作之前，都必须在莱顿住上两年，向荷兰人

When the President stated tonight that Plymouth Rock celebrated this anniversary on the 21st, whilst we here did so on the 22d, he did not state the true reason. It is not as he said, a dispute about dates. The pork and beans of Plymouth are insufficient for the cravings of the Yankee appetite, and they chose the 21st, in order that, by the night train, they may get to New York on the 22d, to have once a year a square meal. From 1620 down to the opening of New York to their settlement, a constantly increasing void was growing inside the Yankee diaphragm, and even now the native and imported Yankee finds the best – appointed restaurant in the world sufficient for his wants; and he has migrated to this house, that he may annually have the sensation of sufficiency in the largest hotel in the United States.

My friend, Mr. Curtis, has eloquently stated, in the beginning of his address, the Dutchman's idea of the old Puritan. He has stated, at the close of his address, the modern opinion of the old Puritan. He was an uncomfortable man to live with, but two hundred years off a grand historic figure. If any one of you, gentlemen, was compelled to leave this festive board, and go back two hundred years and live with your ancestor of that day, eat his fare, drink his drink, and listen to his talk, what a time would be there, my countrymen! Before the Puritan was fitted to accomplish the work he did, with all the great opportunities that were in him, it was necessary that he should spend two years in Leyden and

学习宗教容忍的重要课程以及其他基础课程，因为普通学校教育是建立在公民和宗教完全自由的基础上的。如果当初是荷兰人占领了波士顿，那将是这片土地甚至整个世界的不幸。这就像迪德里克·尼克博克同电池摔跤一样。

但新英格兰人占领了纽约之后，他们同荷兰人的联合形成了造就现在美利坚合众国的坚实基础。在美国参议院里的激烈争论中，新英格兰人的思想在这片土地上占了上风。这种现象已经或将要表现在民族主义对地方主义的胜利上，而这种胜利是伟大的宪法辩护者丹尼尔·韦伯斯特凭借其沉稳的雄辩取得的。当地方主义在论坛上失败后便开始用武器说话，当李将军向联邦军总司令格兰特弃甲投降时，新英格兰人的思想在那次历史性会议上再一次获得胜利。在随后的诚信危机和工业危机中，当扩张和拒付债务的流毒向海外蔓延时，新英格兰思想在我们的贵宾——财政部长的决策中又一次获得胜利，其结果是决定以 4% 的利息支付国债并恢复国家信用。从来没有一位财政部长能赢得过如此巨大的胜利，这极大地鼓励了我们工业的发展和社会的繁荣，而工业与社会前进的步伐是不能停滞不前的。

当亨利·赫德森驾船驶到纽约港口并用预言

learn from the Dutch the important lesson of religious toleration, and the other fundamental lesson, that a common school education lies at the foundation of all civil and religious liberty. If the Dutchman had conquered Boston, it would have been a misfortune to this land, and to the world. It would have been like Diedrich Knickerbocker wrestling with an electric battery.

But when the Yankee conquered New York, his union with the Dutch formed those sterling elements which have made the Republic what it is. Yankee ideas prevailed in this land in the grandest contest in the Senate of the United States which has ever taken place, or ever will, in the victory of Nationalism over Sectionalism by the ponderous eloquence of that great defender of the Constitution, Daniel Webster. And when failing in the forum, Sectionalism took the field, Yankee ideas conquered again in that historic meeting when Lee gave up his sword to Grant. And when, in the disturbance of credit and industry which followed, the twin heresies Expansion and Repudiation stalked abroad, Yankee ideas conquered again in the policy of our distinguished guest, the Secretary of the Treasury. So great a triumph has never been won by any financial officer of the government before, as in the funding of our national debt at four per cent., and the restoration of the national credit, giving an impulse to our prosperity and industry that can neither be stayed nor stopt.

When Henry Hudson sailed up the great

家的眼光看到它巨大的潜力时，他不由得用真正荷兰式的意味深长来强调自己的看法，他说的那句话是："嘿，看吧！"当新英格兰人来到纽约并在此定居后，也曾用另外一句话来强调自己的到来："就留在这儿了。" 新英格兰人用尽全力把荷兰人挤出了白菜地，并在上面兴建了仓库和住宅。新英格兰人曾发现展现在眼前的城市宛如一座由许多养牛场组成的美丽迷宫，迷宫里有居民和山墙全部面向街道的房舍，他们把这一切变成了一条大道，把纽约变成了平行四边形的宫殿。新英格兰人越来越人丁兴旺，如今他们遍布在我们这个州的每个角落。今晚在这儿我们意识到由于新英格兰和纽约之间没有关税，实行的是自由贸易，本土的产品比进口产品质量还要好。先生们，请允许我说，在这个州热情好客、自由精神及世界知名人士的影响之下，作为世世代代居住在这里的纽约本地人，你们已从过去 200 年前不受欢迎的清教徒变成最令人愉快、最友善的人了。

今天的纽约，作为所有伟大的联邦州中的帝国之州，凭借其海路优势承担了共和国 80%的进口和绝大多数的出口贸易，并收取和缴纳了供养

harbor of New York, and saw with prophetic vision its magnificent opportunities, he could only emphasize his thought, with true Dutch significance, in one sentence—"See here!" When the Yankee came and settled in New York, he emphasized his coming with another sentence—"Sit here!"—and he sat down upon the Dutchman with such force that he squeezed him out of his cabbage-patch, and upon it he built his warehouse and his residence. He found this city laid out in a beautiful labyrinth of cow-patches, with the inhabitants and the houses all standing with their gable-ends to the street, and he turned them all to the avenue, and made New York a parallelogram of palaces; and he has multiplied to such an extent that now he fills every nook of our great State, and we recognize here to-night that, with no tariff, and free trade between New England and New York, the native specimen is an improvement upon the imported article. Gentlemen, I beg leave to say, as a native New Yorker of many generations, that by the influence, the hospitality, the liberal spirit, and the cosmopolitan influences of this great State, from the unlovable Puritan of two hundred years ago you have become the most agreeable and companionable of men.

New York today, the Empire State of all the great States of the Commonwealth, brings in through her grand avenue to the sea eighty per cent. Of all the imports, and sends forth a majority of all the exports, of the Republic. She collects and pays four-fifths of the taxes which carry on

国家政府部门的五分之四的税金。 如今竞争激烈,而面向世界的西部贸易正在3000英里的海岸线上寻找出路,为了抓牢西部贸易,纽约凭借其商业威望和企业的优势,掌握着比从新奥尔良到波特兰所有港口总和还要多的海港。不论是本土的还是后迁来的纽约人,让我们坦诚地面对这个商业、金融大都市的过去、现在和未来;让我们扩展码头设施的规模,将铁路和轮船运输发展成一条龙模式;让我们消除使纽约成为收费最高港口的负担,使其成为北美洲最廉价的港口;让我们的商业思想被国家的立法机关所接受,从而废除共和国的商业船只不可出海的航海法规。让共和国的旗帜在世界各地和各个海域迎风飘扬。

注: 在纽约市新英格兰协会七十四周年宴会上昌西·迪普所做的演讲。

the government of the country. In the close competition to secure the great Western commerce which is today feeding the world and seeking an outlet along three thousand miles of coast, she holds by her commercial prestige and enterprise more than all the ports from New Orleans to Portland combined. Let us, whether native or adopted New Yorkers, be true to the past, to the present, to the future, of this commercial and financial metropolis. Let us enlarge our terminal facilities and bring the rail and the steamship close together. Let us do away with the burdens that make New York the dearest, and make her the cheapest, port on the continent; and let us impress our commercial ideas upon the national legislature, so that the navigation laws, which have driven the merchant marine of the Republic from the seas, shall be repealed, and the breezes of every clime shall unfurl, and the waves of every sea reflect, the flag of the Republic.

FOOTNOTE:
Speech of Chauncey M. Depew at the seventy-fourth anniversary banquet of the New England Society in the City of New York.

11.

文人雅士

詹姆斯·安东尼·弗劳德[1]

弗兰西斯·格兰特爵士、殿下、

阁下们和各位先生：

当您把我的名字与文学界联系在一起时，我真切地感受到您给予我的荣幸。然而对于我演讲主题的实质，我又觉得惶恐不安。什么是文学？什么是文人雅士？从某种角度看，我们是人类中最没有用的，总是在吹肥皂泡。从另一个角度看，我们又是社会中最实际、最精力充沛的一部分。如果说文学是为阐述事实、表达思想情感而巧妙地遣词造句的一门艺术，那么每天见诸报端的广告便是

---

①1818～1894，英国历史学家，小说家，传记作家。

11.

Men of Letters

By James Anthony Froude

Sir Francis Grant, Your Royal Highness,
My Lords, and Gentlemen:

While I feel most keenly the honor which you confer upon me in connecting my name with the interests of literature, I am embarrassed, in responding, by the nature of my subject. What is literature, and who are men of letters? From one point of view we are the most unprofitable of mankind—engaged mostly in blowing soap-bubbles. From another point of view we are the most practical and energetic portion of the community. If literature be the art of employing words skilfully in representing facts, or thoughts, or emotions, you may see excellent specimens of it every day in the

我们看得到的出色的实例。每个利用手中的笔向他人传达自己思想的人都属于文人的范畴，如科学家、商人和学者。不，他甚至不需要用笔。优秀演讲家的演讲即是每个国家文学中的奇葩。在美国格拉顿先生的演讲词是修辞学校的教科书，而布赖特先生在演讲方面的造诣使他在英国文人中占有最重要的地位。

每一个杰出的人不论他的职业是什么，也不论他是否具备儒雅的气质，只要他足够出色，只要他在国人心目中占有举足轻重的位置，都可能成为我们中的一员。即便不是在他活着的时候，那么他辞世后也将被吸收进我们的行列。人们迫切地想了解他人生的经历，而这些好奇心总能得到满足。人们搜寻他的信件，挑选他的日记，将他说过的话及写给兄弟姐妹的打油诗结集出版。这是命运使然，他无从摆脱。我们大声抱怨，然而看来人们并不真心抵制这样的肆意胡闹。我们从没听说过他们曾吩咐遗嘱执行人烧毁自己的书信与文件。因为，他们仍很喜欢让自己的同代人出出洋相，于是也就甘心做点自我牺牲了。

再者，先生们，我们在哪儿能找到通常意义上

advertisements in our newspapers. Every man who uses a pen to convey his meaning to others—the man of science, the man of business, the member of a learned profession—belongs to the community of letters. Nay, he need not use his pen at all. The speeches of great orators are among the most treasured features of any national literature. The orations of Mr. Grattan are the text-books in the schools of rhetoric in the United States. Mr. Bright, under this aspect of him, holds a foremost place among the men of letters of England.

Again, sir, every eminent man, be he what he will, be he as unbookish as he pleases, so he is only eminent enough, so he holds a conspicuous place in the eyes of his countrymen, potentially belongs to us, and if not in life, then after he is gone, will be enrolled among us. The public insist on being admitted to his history, and their curiosity will not go unsatisfied. His letters are hunted up, his journals are sifted; his sayings in conversation, the doggerel which he writes to his brothers and sisters are collected, and stereotyped in print. His fate overtakes him. He can not escape from it. We cry out, but it does not appear that men sincerely resist the liberty which is taken with them. We never hear of them instructing their executors to burn their papers. They have enjoyed so much the exhibition that has been made of their contemporaries that they consent to be sacrificed themselves.

Again, sir, when we look for those who have been most distinguished as men of letters, in the

杰出的文人雅士呢？我们在事务所可以找到著名的律师，在工作室中可以找到著名的艺术家。文人雅士的杰出代表并不总是待在自己的书斋里，我们发现他们首先是在为祖国效劳。（“说得对！说得好！”）欧文·梅雷迪思是印度的殖民总督，全英国一致赞成把他选派到印度的决定。三年前曾卓有成效地管理国家的令人钦佩的人（格莱斯顿先生）是以优秀作家的身份首先被国人广泛熟知的。他在四十年艰难的从政期间仍然没有放弃他最初的职业，总是利用间歇的空闲时间为英国人民翻译荷马的著作，并同最负盛名的神学家们争辩以维护精神自由。

近来我们一直在饶有兴趣地阅读一位伟大作家的生平故事，而这位作家推断到公元 3000 年仍会有人研读他的作品。假使任何人在当代人的赞扬声中都难免对自己产生这样的期望，那么麦考利勋爵则可被认为并没有这样的虚荣心。公元 3000 年离我们还很遥远，在此期间还会有许多事情发生，我们只能肯定地说公元 3000 年将同我们任何人的预想都相去甚远。我不想预测那时人们会不会阅读麦考利勋爵的《英国历史》，也不愿去

usual sense of the word, where do we find them? The famous lawyer is found in his chambers, the famous artist is found in his studio. Our foremost representatives we do not find always in their libraries; we find them, in the first place, in the service of their country. ("Hear! Hear!") Owen Meredith is Viceroy of India, and all England has applauded the judgment that selected and sent him there. The right honorable gentleman (Mr. Gladstone) who three years ago was conducting the administration of this country with such brilliant success was first generally known to his countrymen as a remarkable writer. During forty years of arduous service he never wholly deserted his original calling. He is employing an interval of temporary retirement to become the interpreter of Homer to the English race, or to break a lance with the most renowned theologians in defense of spiritual liberty.

A great author, whose life we have been all lately reading with delight, contemplates the year 3000 as a period at which his works may still be studied. If any man might be led reasonably to form such an anticipation for himself by the admiration of his contemporaries, Lord Macaulay may be acquitted of vanity. The year 3000 is far away, much will happen between now and then; all that we can say with certainty of the year 3000 is that it will be something extremely different from what any one expects. I will not predict that men will then be reading Lord Macaulay's "History of England." I will not predict that they will then

设想他们是否会读《洛泰尔》。但我要说的是,迪斯累里先生在其著作《洛泰尔》中描绘了部分英国社会,倘若奥古斯都大帝或安东尼时代的政治家们能够像他一样以形象的手法和巧妙的讽刺对罗马贵族的生活为我们进行过描绘的话,我们就不会对那些古代遗迹如痴如醉地仔细研究了。因此,我们是一个难以界定的特殊群体。尽管如此,我们仍然对各位给予的祝福表达由衷的感激,请接受我最忠心的谢意!

be reading "Lothair." But this I will say, that if any statesman of the age of Augustus or the Antonines had left us a picture of patrician society at Rome, drawn with the same skill, and with the same delicate irony with which Mr. Disraeli has described a part of English society in "Lothair," no relic of antiquity would now be devoured with more avidity and interest. Thus, sir, we are an anomalous body, with very ill-defined limits. But, such as we are, we are heartily obliged to you for wishing us well, and I give you our most sincere thanks.

12.

文学和政治

约翰·莫利[1]

尊敬的总统先生、尊敬的殿下，
阁下们、女士们、先生们：

在当代知识界和社交界名流出席的这次盛大聚会上，我觉得自己现在比八年前更不够资格担当文学界的代表了。我还不能像首相那样在展览厅里转一圈，去看墙上光彩夺目的艺术作品。但是在首相的建议下我打算去看包括罗什福尔在内的自由党领袖们的肖像。虽然我不确定罗什福尔是文学家还是自由党的领袖，但我知道他的肖像之

①1838～1923，英国自由党议员，作家，报社编辑。

12.

Literature and Politics

By John Morley

Mr. President, Your Royal Highness,
My Lords, Ladies and Gentlemen:

I feel that I am more unworthy now than I was eight years ago to figure as the representative of literature before this brilliant gathering of all the most important intellectual and social interests of our time. I have not yet been able like the Prime Minister, to go round this exhibition and see the works of art that glorify your walls; but I am led by him to expect that I shall see the pictures of Liberal leaders, including M. Rochefort. I am not sure whether M. Rochefort will figure as a man of letters or as a Liberal leader, but I can understand that his portrait would attract the Prime Minister

所以吸引首相是因为，他是位曾经当过自由党领袖的政治家，而且他现在有理由可以不再信任议会政体了。我也没看到“涨潮”那幅画，但我想当我真正见到它时，我可能会在画中看到许多的更衣车。我想在更衣车中无论老幼肯定都在满怀信心地等待——等待“涨潮”的到来。当它到来时，那些被囚禁在这些更衣车中的老先生们一定都十分渴望有人骑马来，将他们从即将到来的危险中解救出去。

总统先生，在您祝酒词的末尾，我感到了淡淡的责备的语气，您责备人们因为社会生活中的混乱与无限竞争而放弃高尚愉快的文学。我认为现在文学和社会分离的程度比以往任何一个时代都严重。在女王时代有两位著名的政治家，他们都以曾三次出任首相而闻名于世。说来也怪，他们中的一位（德比勋爵）在身后留下了生气盈盈的荷马史诗译本，而另外一位杰出的政治家威廉·格莱斯顿（幸运的是他现在还和我们在一起），仍然在研究荷马史诗的传说和它的重要意义。然后，我们再回顾一下距离现在较近的一段时期。在最近六年的爱尔兰政府内阁中，我发现至少有 3 位（乔治·

because M. Rochefort is a politician who was once a Liberal leader, and who has now seen occasion to lose his faith in Parliamentary government. Nor have I seen the picture of "The Flowing Tide," but I shall expect to find in that picture when I do see it a number of bathing-machines in which, not the younger generation, but the elder generation, as I understand are waiting confidently—for the arrival of the "Flowing Tide," and when it arrives, the elderly gentlemen who are incarcerated in those machines will be only too anxious for a man and a horse to come and deliver them from their imminent peril.

I thought that I detected in the last words of your speech, in proposing this toast, Mr. President, an accent of gentle reproach that any one should desert the high and pleasant ways of literature for the turmoil and the everlasting contention of public life. I do not suppose that there has ever been a time in which there was less of divorce between literature and public life than the present time. There have been in the reign of the Queen two eminent statesmen who have thrice had the distinction of being Prime Minister, and oddly enough, one of those statesman (Lord Derby) has left behind him a most spirited version of Homer, while the other eminent statesman (William E. Gladstone)—happily still among us, still examines the legends and the significance of Homer. Then when we come to a period nearer to ourselves, and look at those gentlemen who have in the last six years filled the office of Minister for Ireland,

奥托·特里维廉，约翰·莫利和阿瑟·鲍尔弗）在致力于棘手的政府事务之前都曾著书立说。他们之中的一位在开始自己的文学生涯时（这带给了他极高的荣誉），还得到了三人中另外一位的支持，而那另一位当时是编辑。在立法机关中，我们有一位妙笔生花的传记作家。我们还有另外一位作家（詹姆斯·布赖斯），他的知识面和学术兴趣十分广泛，他撰写过一部关于美国联邦政体的重要作品。

文学的第一个准则是100年前一位著名的法国人宣布的，他说在文学中你可以有优先权，却没有排他权。在政治中，我们似乎坚决要拥有不可改变的优先权，而在生活中排他权则是我们的一贯目标之一。在文学中，根据另一条准则，你必须有自由的、开放的头脑，因此才有人说："不要囚禁在你自己的观点中。"在政治中，如果你没有倒霉地成为别人观点的囚徒，那已经是十分幸运了（我想坐在总统两边的先生们都会认可这个观点）。当然，没有人会怀疑文学的伟大成就（即我们永远也不会让其消失的那些永恒的重要著作）需要一种持久的、耐心的、不倦的忠诚，正如装饰在墙壁上

we find that no fewer than three (George Otto Trevelyan, John Morley, and Arthur Balfour) were authors of books before they engaged in the very ticklish business of the government of men. And one of these three Ministers for Ireland embarked upon his literary career—which promised ample distinction—under the editorial auspices of another of the three. We possess in one branch of the Legislature the author of the most fascinating literary biography in our language. We possess also another writer whose range of knowledge and of intellectual interest is so great that he has written the most important book upon the American Commonwealth (James Bryce).

The first canon in literature was announced one hundred years ago by an eminent Frenchman who said that in literature it is your business to have preferences but no exclusions. In politics it appears to be our business to have very stiff and unchangeable preferences, and exclusion is one of the systematic objects of our life. In literature, according to another canon, you must have a free and open mind and it has been said: "Never be the prisoner of your own opinions." In politics you are very lucky if you do not have the still harder fate—(and I think that the gentlemen on the President's right hand will assent to that as readily as the gentlemen who sit on his left) of being the prisoner of other people's opinions. Of course no one can doubt for a moment that the great achievements of literature—those permanent and vital works which we will never let die—require a devotion as unceasing, as patient, as inexhaustible,

的美术作品需要的忠诚那样。在我们这个时代里——虽然它可能不是一个文学的时代——我们很幸运地拥有散文巨匠和诗歌大师。没有哪篇散文像纽曼主教的散文那样动人，没有哪首诗歌比丁尼生勋爵和斯温伯恩先生的诗歌更优美、更华丽、更有音乐的韵味了。

在我看来，现代文学最重要的功能之一不仅是要创作鸿篇巨制，而且是要捍卫英语语言，捍卫这种卓越而光辉灿烂的交流工具，使其免受当前出现的大量外来语的侵犯。我相信今天在场的每个人肯定都注意到了最近提出的用来称呼电子运动的名称，这些名称有一长串，这一长串名词揭示了一个我们许多人早已察觉到的事实，也就是说存在着某些时刻要玷污和破坏我们母语的可怕力量。这些奇异的、怪诞的、可笑的、荒唐的名称预示着一幅非常讨厌的前景。当美国报纸在头版头条吹捧的幽默作家将作为简洁、活泼、生动风格的典范而走红时，我担心那一天正在逼近（我不敢肯定它是不是正在步步逼近）。

即使在我们的讲演中，那些外来词汇入侵的程度也是让人震惊的。假如十七世纪的清教徒们获悉他们十九世纪的子孙们来这儿出差，还顺便

as the devotion that is required for the works that adorn your walls; and we have luckily in our age—tho it may not be a literary age—masters of prose and masters of verse. No prose more winning has ever been written than that of Cardinal Newman; no verse finer, more polished, more melodious has ever been written than that of Lord Tennyson and Mr. Swinburne.

It seems to me that one of the greatest functions of literature at this moment is not merely to produce great works, but also to protect the English language—that noble, that most glorious instrument—against those hosts of invaders which I observe have in these days sprung up. I suppose that every one here has noticed the extraordinary list of names suggested lately in order to designate motion by electricity; that list of names only revealed what many of us had been observing for a long time—namely, the appalling forces that are ready at a moment's notice to deface and deform our English tongue. These strange, fantastic, grotesque, and weird titles open up to my prophetic vision a most unwelcome prospect. I tremble to see the day approach—and I am not sure that it is not approaching—when the humorists of the headlines of American journalism shall pass current as models of conciseness, energy, and color of style.

Even in our social speech this invasion seems to be taking place in an alarming degree, and I wonder what the Pilgrim Fathers of the seventeenth century would say if they could hear

"On the make"(发点洋财)时,我不知道他们会怎么说。而"On the make"只是成千上万怪诞说法中的一个，正是它们在破坏着我们语言中清教徒式的纯洁。站在我自己的角度,我只想说,我希望在所有的图书馆和报社中都能看到弥尔顿那段令人赞叹的名言——弥尔顿懂得如何运用好散文这种伟大的工具和诗歌这种高尚的工具。他在那段名言中宣称他不但欣赏那种提供勇气和无畏的忠告去反击敌人的人，也欣赏那些召集一些优秀作家抵制不规范语言侵入人们的思维与讲话方式、说话与写作习惯的人。

感谢大家让我很荣幸地谈了谈有关最幸福的职业和最不朽的作品的话题。

their pilgrim children of the nineteenth century who come over here, on various missions, and among others, "On the make." This is only one of the thousand such-like expressions which are invading the Puritan simplicity of our tongue. I will only say that I should like, for my own part, to see in every library and in every newspaper office that admirable passage in which Milton—who knew so well how to handle both the great instrument of prose and the nobler instrument of verse—declared that next to the man who furnished courage and intrepid counsels against an enemy he placed the man who should enlist small bands of good authors to resist that barbarism which invades the minds and the speech of men in methods and habits of speaking and writing.

I thank you for having allowed me the honor of saying a word as to the happiest of all callings and the most imperishable of all arts.

13.

谢尔曼将军

卡尔·舒尔茨[1]

先生们：

商会通过的这些决议不仅仅是例行公事，我完全支持。一种情不自禁的真情将我们召集到这里。对于我们来说，谢尔曼将军的伟大和其他让人敬而远之的伟人不同。我们可以骄傲和高兴地把他当作我们中的一员。就在几个月前，我们还在商会的年度会议中见过我们名誉会员那张熟悉的脸，他坐在台上，会长的旁边。就在几周前，他还像

①1829～1906，美国议员，改革家，美国南北战争期间联合军上将。

13.

General Sherman

By Carl Schurz

Gentlemen:

The adoption by the Chamber of Commerce of these resolutions which I have the honor to second, is no mere perfunctory proceeding. We have been called here by a genuine impulse of the heart. To us General Sherman was not a great man like other great men, honored and revered at a distance. We had the proud and happy privilege of calling him one of us. Only a few months ago, at the annual meeting of this Chamber, we saw the familiar face of our honorary member on this platform by the side of our President. Only a few weeks ago he sat at our banquet table, as he had

平常一样快乐地坐在宴会的餐桌旁，用一贯谦虚而富有魅力的演讲为那个晚上带来了许多欢乐。他徜徉于宾客之中，对于过去的光荣历史没有丝毫的夸耀，表现出来的只有热情和亲切，我们都很难想象他曾经是一代名将，曾率领着强大的军队打过很多胜仗。他的名字屹立在，并将会永远屹立在共和国功臣的最前列，屹立在世界历史上名将的最前列。事实上，所有的美国人一刻也不会忘记这些，而那些有幸和他接近的人们对他的情感已经超过了感激和崇拜。

最终死神战胜了这位身经百战的英雄，全国的城市、乡镇和农村都降半旗致哀。他的遗体入殓时，沉闷的鼓声和隆隆的葬礼的炮声在整个大地上回响。美国人民将满怀悲痛地忍受着这位伟人突然逝去而留下的空虚。他是为民族的新生而战的伟人中的最后一位，也是除了亚布拉罕·林肯之外最后一位最广泛地受到人们爱戴的人。他已经离去了，但是就像我们这代人将牢记他“向海上进军”的著名传奇一样，历史也会向后世讲述这段传奇：在 1864 年那些黑暗的日子里，谢尔曼杀出了

often before, in the happiest mood of conviviality, and contributed to the enjoyment of the night with his always unassuming and always charming speech. And as he moved among us without the slightest pomp of self-conscious historic dignity, only with the warm and simple geniality of his nature, it would cost us sometimes an effort of the memory to recollect that he was the renowned captain who had marshaled mighty armies victoriously on many a battlefield, and whose name stood, and will forever stand, in the very foremost rank of the saviors of this Republic, and of the great soldiers of the world's history. Indeed, no American could have forgotten this for a moment; but the affection of those who were so happy as to come near to him, would sometimes struggle to outrun their veneration and gratitude.

Death has at last conquered the hero of so many campaigns; our cities and towns and villages are decked with flags at half-mast; the muffled drum and the funeral cannon boom will resound over the land as his dead body passes to the final resting-place; and the American people stand mournfully gazing into the void left by the sudden disappearance of the last of the greatest men brought forth by our war of regeneration—and this last also finally become, save Abraham Lincoln alone, the most widely beloved. He is gone; but as we of the present generation remember it, history will tell all coming centuries the romantic story of the famous "March to the Sea"—how, in the dark days of 1864, Sherman, having worked his bloody

一条血路扑向亚特兰大，然后他切断所有供给线和通讯联系，就像勇敢的潜水员潜入了黑暗的未知水域一样，他和自己的部队好像从世人的视线里消失了，直到他们胜利地出现在海岸上，向无数焦急等待的人们宣告了：现在最后的胜利已毋庸置疑，共和国一定会得救。

历史也不会忘记这位伟大的将军不仅是一名战无不胜的战士，也是共和国公民的楷模。取得了许多杰出成绩后，他一步一步升到了军队的最高职位，然后年老退休。共和国以自己的方式为他的退休生活做了比较简单的安排，但他很满足，他没有要求更高的报酬。虽然每个士兵都带着他辉煌的成就和对他的爱回到了各自的家中——这使他成为那个时代在美国最受欢迎的人，虽然最耀眼的奖章经常展现在他的眼前，但是他却始终心平气和。他从来没有想过共和国是否欠了他太多，因此他总是心情豁朗，即便有人跟他说“共和国忘恩负义”，也总是受到他严厉的训斥。所以他能够因为自己杰出地履行了崇高的职责而知足，因为受到同胞们的爱戴而高兴。

事实上，可以真切地说，在他晚年的时候，他不仅是最受人爱戴的人，还是全美国最快乐的人。他有很多年是和子孙们住在一起的。他很清楚，他的任务已经完成了。他的功绩已由历史作出评判，

way to Atlanta, then cast off all his lines of supply and communication, and, like a bold diver into the dark unknown, seemed to vanish with all his hosts from the eyes of the world, until his triumphant reappearance on the shores of the ocean proclaimed to the anxiously expecting millions, that now the final victory was no longer doubtful, and that the Republic would surely be saved.

Nor will history fail to record that this great general was, as a victorious soldier, a model of republican citizenship. When he had done his illustrious deeds, he rose step by step to the highest rank in the army, and then, grown old, he retired. The Republic made provision for him in modest republican style. He was satisfied. He asked for no higher reward. Altho the splendor of his achievements, and the personal affection for him, which every one of his soldiers carried home, made him the most popular American of his day, and altho the most glittering prizes were not seldom held up before his eyes, he remained untroubled by ulterior ambition. No thought that the Republic owed him more ever darkened his mind. No man could have spoken to him of the "ingratitude of Republics," without meeting from him a stern rebuke. And so, content with the consciousness of a great duty nobly done, he was happy in the love of his fellow citizens.

Indeed, he may truly be said to have been in his old age, not only the most beloved, but also the happiest of Americans. Many years he lived in the midst of posterity. His task was finished, and

已经确定地记录在祖国和时代的辉煌中。他胸怀宽广，从不嫉妒别人，希望每个人都幸福，怨恨早已经和他无缘。他的声望是无可挑剔的。他不胜欣慰地享受着自己磊落地赢得的名望，他那坦诚的性情即是对这一点的公开昭示。他很高兴收到同胞们尊重和珍视；他所最看重的声誉，在他日趋衰老的岁月里一直有增无减。因此他真的是最快乐的人，他的日子过得就像秋天里万里无云的天空中的夕阳一样灿烂。现在，美国人一如既往地怀着对他的那种特殊的爱戴将这位伟人安葬。他是快乐地走到他生命的终点的，这也许能给那些悲痛万分的同胞们一些安慰吧。他们为失去这样一位敬爱的老英雄而悲痛。他们过去以他为骄傲，并且将来也会永远以他为骄傲。我们将永远缅怀他的光辉形象。他真正的纪念碑就是他为之作出不朽贡献的伟大的共和国，他的英名将作为十分宝贵的财富永远被怀着感激之情的全国人民铭记。

this he wisely understood. His deeds had been passed upon by the judgment of history, and irrevocably registered among the glories of his country and his age. His generous heart envied no one, and wished every one well; and ill-will had long ceased to pursue him. Beyond cavil his fame was secure, and he enjoyed it as that which he had honestly earned, with a genuine and ever fresh delight, openly avowed by the charming frankness of his nature. He dearly loved to be esteemed and cherished by his fellow men, and what he valued most, his waning years brought him in ever increasing abundance. Thus he was in truth a most happy man, and his days went down like an evening sun in a cloudless autumn sky. And when now the American people, with that peculiar tenderness of affection which they have long borne him, lay him in his grave, the happy ending of his great life may soothe the pang of bereavement they feel in their hearts at the loss of the old hero who was so dear to them, and of whom they were and always will be so proud. His memory will ever be bright to us all; his truest monument will be the greatness of the Republic he served so well; and his fame will never cease to be prized by a grateful country, as one of its most precious possessions.

14.

为亚历山大·汉密尔顿所致的悼词

古弗尼尔·莫里斯[①]

朋友们：

在这样一个悲痛肃穆的时刻，如果我还竭力地唤起大家的惋惜之情，这显然对大家已经普遍而真实地表达出来的感受是不公平的。我非但不想使大家情绪激动，我还会努力控制住自己的情绪。但是，恐怕你们将要听到的不是一个演讲家的演讲，而是一个悲痛的朋友的哀悼。不过，我将尽力控制住自己悲痛欲绝的心情，来追述那已经升入天国的英灵的英雄业绩。

哥伦比亚大学的同学们，当他跟你们一样正在安宁的校园里热切地追求知识时，独立战争的

①1752～1816，美国议员，美国宪法起草人之一。

14.

Oration over Alexander Hamilton

By Gouverneur Morris

My Friends:

If on this sad, this solemn occasion, I should endeavor to move your commiseration, it would be doing injustice to that sensibility which has been so generally and so justly manifested. Far from attempting to excite your emotions, I must try to repress my own; and yet, I fear, that instead of the language of a public speaker, you will hear only the lamentations of a wailing friend. But I will struggle with my bursting heart, to portray that heroic spirit, which has flown to the mansions of bliss.

Students of Columbia—he was in the ardent pursuit of knowledge in your academic shades

第一声炮响将他召唤到了战场。那时他是一个义无反顾的年轻志愿兵，满腔热情、英勇善战，在我们还不认识他时，就已经听到了他的名字。好像是上帝创造出这么一个人来帮助拯救这个世界。华盛顿敏锐的目光发现了激荡在他年轻的胸膛中的英雄气概。正所谓慧眼识珠，他被华盛顿选为副官，于是，他开始进入人们的视线，并成为那场革命战争中许多重要战役中的主要角色。在围攻约克城时，他不屈不挠地当上了一支敢死队的队长。他猛攻据点，但创造了没有一个敌人死亡的记录。在他的英雄气概的带动下，勇敢的部队将抬起的枪口又放了下去，饶恕了不再抵抗的敌人。在那里，他结束了自己的戎马生涯。

战争结束后不久，你们的厚爱，不，是你们锐利的眼光将他调到政府部门工作。你们派他去了费城的国会，在那里他帮助制定了宪法，那部宪法现在已经成为了我们国家的基本大法，是我们安全的盾牌，是我们繁荣昌盛的源泉。在签署宪法时，他表达了自己的担忧，他担心宪法缺乏有力的手段维护自己，担心我们的命运结果可能和其他共和国一样，从无政府状态走向专制统治。我们希望情况更好一些。我们相信美国人民是明智的，更重要的是，我们相信保佑我们的万能上帝。在这个

when the first sound of the American war called him to the field. A young and unprotected volunteer, such was his zeal, and so brilliant his service, that we heard his name before we knew his person. It seemed as if God had called him suddenly into existence, that he might assist to save a world! The penetrating eye of Washington soon perceived the manly spirit which animated his youthful bosom. By that excellent judge of men he was selected as an aid, and thus he became early acquainted with, and was a principal actor in the more important scenes of our revolution. At the siege of York he pertinaciously insisted on, and he obtained the command of a Forlorn Hope. He stormed the redoubt; but let it be recorded that not one single man of the enemy perished. His gallant troops, emulating the heroism of their chief checked the uplifted arm, and spared a foe no longer resisting. Here closed his military career.

Shortly after the war, your favor—no, your discernment, called him to public office. You sent him to the convention at Philadelphia; he there assisted in forming the constitution which is now the bond of our union, the shield of our defense, and the source of our prosperity. In signing the compact, he exprest his apprehension that it did not contain sufficient means of strength for its own preservation; and that in consequence we should share the fate of many other republics, and pass through anarchy to despotism. We hoped better things. We confided in the good sense of the American people; and, above all, we trusted in the

重要的问题上,他从来没有隐瞒过自己的观点,他鄙视遮遮掩掩的态度。他认定自己心无私念,所以他能把自己的心像捧在手上一样向所有的人亮出其最深处的东西。他的豪爽和轻率使他遭受过许多歪曲的指责。他的理论观点被认为是精心设计的,但是我们都知道他是如何竭尽全力地、不懈地制定和维护宪法的。即使他的观点是错误的,那么,请原谅他吧,原谅他这唯一的错误,他在为大家服务的一生中那唯一的错误吧。

在我们的政府刚刚成立的时候,尽管我们不乏资源却没有资金。为了开发利用资源并且建立金融秩序,华盛顿四处寻求杰出的人才和各种信息,更重要的是他要找到廉洁正直的管理者。他发现汉密尔顿具备了全部条件。汉密尔顿提出的金融制度后来被采纳了,却一直受到诸多批评。即使那制度有缺陷,可是人们不应忘记金无足赤、人无完人。回想一下当时的环境,回想一下那时意见的冲突,而且,尤其重要的是,不要忘记一个共和国的部长必须将就人民的意愿。华盛顿建立的政府是非常有效率、非常优秀的政府,无论哪个国家有这样的政府都应该感到荣幸。结果,我们的国家很快地强大和昌盛起来了。这在其他任何时代、任何国家都是没有先例的。汉密尔顿在其中的贡献也是世人皆知的。

protecting providence of the Almighty. On this important subject he never concealed his opinion. He disdained concealment. Knowing the purity of his heart, he bore it as it were in his hand, exposing to every passenger its inmost recesses. This generous indiscretion subjected him to censure from misrepresentation. His speculative opinions were treated as deliberate designs; and yet you all know how strenuous, how unremitting were his efforts to establish and to preserve the constitution. If, then, his opinion was wrong, pardon, O pardon, that single error, in a life devoted to your service.

At the time when our Government was organized, we were without funds, tho not without resources. To call them into action, and establish order in the finances, Washington sought for splendid talents, for extensive information, and above all, he sought for sterling, incorruptible integrity. All these he found in Hamilton. The system then adopted, has been the subject of much animadversion. If it be not without a fault, let it be remembered that nothing human is perfect. Recollect the circumstances of the moment—recollect the conflict of opinion—and, above all, remember that a minister of a republic must bend to the will of the people. The administration which Washington formed was one of the most efficient, one of the best that any country was ever blessed with. And the result was a rapid advance in power and prosperity of which there is no example in any other age or nation. The part which Hamilton bore is universally known.

他会毫不怀疑地相信别人的表白，相信那些表白都是真诚的，这使他过于相信了一些不值得信任的人,从而又使他受到另一些人的误解。他觉得自己不得不辞职了。家庭人口的增加和有限的家底使他感到有责任去重操旧业以养家糊口。但是,虽然他被迫离开了公务员的岗位,却从未放弃过为公众服务。他始终在关注大家的利益。我可以面对上帝郑重地对大家说，即便在最私密的谈话中，他讨论和思考的唯一问题也是大家的自由和幸福。大家一定还清楚地记得华盛顿第二次出山率领军队时的情形，大家知道华盛顿曾请求汉密尔顿作他的副统帅。这位可敬的伟人非常清楚戎马生涯的凶险，他感到了时间之手在挤压生命之源。他可能很快殒身沙场，他的副手将继承指挥权。凭经验他知道这个位置的重要性,他认为可以把美国之剑安全地委托给现在正躺在冰冷的棺木中的这个人的手中。噢,我的同胞们,请记住这是他没有野心的庄严证明，但他总是被指责野心勃勃,也因此深受这种诋毁的伤害。在他交出自己的指挥权时，胸怀坦荡的他宣布自己将不再接受任

His unsuspecting confidence in professions, which he believed to be sincere, led him to trust too much to the undeserving. This exposed him to misrepresentation. He felt himself obliged to resign. The care of a rising family, and the narrowness of his fortune, made it a duty to return to his profession for their support. But tho he was compelled to abandon public life, never, no, never for a moment did he abandon the public service. He never lost sight of your interests. I declare to you, before that God in whose presence we are now especially assembled, that in his most private and confidential conversations, the single objects of discussion and consideration were your freedom and happiness. You well remember the state of things which again called forth Washington from his retreat to lead your armies. You know that he asked for Hamilton to be his second in command. That venerable sage knew well the dangerous incidents of a military profession, and he felt the hand of time pinching life at its source. It was probable that he would soon be removed from the scene, and that his second would succeed to the command. He knew by experience the importance of that place—and he thought the sword of America might safely be confided to the hand which now lies cold in that coffin. Oh! My fellow citizens, remember this solemn testimonial that he was not ambitious. Yet he was charged with ambition, and, wounded by the imputation, when he laid down his command he declared in the proud independence of his soul, that he never

何职务，除非外敌入侵时他应召为保护祖国而奉献自己的生命。这个决定是不可改变的。他的观点和决定决不变更，这就是他的不足。他目标坚定，对有人指责他谋权图利感到愤怒。他只对荣誉满怀热望，但他也深切地牵挂着大家。他无所畏惧，但他却害怕坏人可能用虚伪的表白来赢得你们的信任，并利用这种信任给你们带来灭顶之灾。

辛辛那提的兄弟们，这里躺着我们的领袖！让他永远作为我们的楷模吧。像他一样，在长年累月忠诚地担任公职以后，快乐地履行个人生活中的社会责任吧。啊，他是那么温和与慈祥，他从不冒犯别人，也从不搞欺诈。他宽厚的双手和心灵是向所有人敞开的。

律师界的先生们，你们失去了为律师界增添异彩的人物。珍惜并学习他的榜样吧。像他一样，带着满腔正义和可歌可泣的热忱为当事人谋利益。像他那样坚持永恒的正义原则。

同胞们，大家早已见证了他在事业中的能力，感觉到了他无与伦比的雄辩才能。大家都知道他出色地履行了公民的义务，他从不通过阿谀奉承或牺牲自己的公正原则来讨得大家的欢心。大家也曾见识过他与您据理力争，可是却在您不知不觉中维护了您的利益。现在大家可以感觉到或者

would accept any office, unless in a foreign war he should be called on to expose his life in defense of his country. This determination was immovable. It was his fault that his opinions and his resolutions could not be changed. Knowing his own firm purpose, he was indignant at the charge that he sought for place or power. He was ambitious only for glory, but he was deeply solicitous for you. For himself he feared nothing; but he feared that bad men might, by false professions, acquire your confidence, and abuse it to your ruin.

Brethren of the Cincinnati—there lies our chief! Let him still be our model. Like him, after long and faithful public services, let us cheerfully perform the social duties of private life. Oh! He was mild and gentle. In him there was no offense; no guile. His generous hand and heart were open to all.

Gentlemen of the bar—you have lost your brightest ornament. Cherish and imitate his example. While, like him, with justifiable and laudable zeal, you pursue the interests of your clients, remember, like him, the eternal principle of justice.

Fellow citizens—you have long witnessed his professional conduct, and felt his unrivaled eloquence. You know how well he performed the duties of a citizen—you know that he never courted your favor by adulation or the sacrifice of his own judgment. You have seen him contending against you, and saving your dearest interests, as it were, in spite of yourselves. And you now feel and

说享受到他坚定有力的论证带来的好处了。这也证明我这位已经离去的朋友是值得大家永远怀念的。我要求大家保护他的荣誉。这是他留下的全部——是这些可怜的孤儿可以从父亲那里继承到的一切。但是，同胞们，这荣誉同样也会是你们的宝贵财富。让它来测验那些讨好你们的人吧，你们别听他们的表白而要看他们的品行，在有怀疑的时候要问一问："汉密尔顿会这样做吗？"

大家都知道他是怎么死的。我不能，绝不能描述他最后的情景，这会激起过于强烈的感情，有碍于大家更清醒的判断。别让你们的愤怒引起任何可能再次冒犯法律尊严的行动。站在他的角度上，我来替他说句话吧(因为大家再也听不到他的声音了)：我请求大家尊重自己。

现在，永恒的上帝的牧师们，行使你们神圣的职责吧，把我们逝去的兄弟的骨灰送入灵柩吧！

注：由政治家与实干家古弗尔·莫里斯在纽约市三一教堂门前为亚历山大·汉密尔顿所致的悼词。

enjoy the benefits resulting from the firm energy of his conduct. Bear this testimony to the memory of my departed friend. I charge you to protect his fame. It is all he has left—all that these poor orphan children will inherit from their father. But, my countrymen, that fame may be a rich treasure to you also. Let it be the test by which to examine those who solicit your favor. Disregarding professions, view their conduct, and on a doubtful occasion ask, "Would Hamilton have done this thing?"

You all know how he perished. On this last scene I can not, I must not dwell. It might excite emotions too strong for your better judgment. Suffer not your indignation to lead to any act which might again offend the insulted majesty of the laws. On his part, as from his lips, tho with my voice—for his voice you will hear no more—let me entreat you to respect yourselves.

And now, ye ministers of the everlasting God, perform your holy office, and commit these ashes of our departed brother to the bosom of the grave.

FOOTNOTE:
Funeral oration by Gouverneur Morris, statesman and man of affairs, pronounced before the porch of Trinity Church, New York City, over the body of Alexander Hamilton, just prior to the interment.

15.

悼念麦金利

格罗弗·克利夫兰[1]

他刚刚被美国人民选出来代表他们的国家去维持、保护和捍卫宪法,去为了人民的利益而忠实地执行法令,去维护共和国的荣誉与完整,可是就在今天他的遗体已经安葬了。他的任期结束了,不是因为任期已满,而是因为发生了被刺杀的悲剧。他从此离开了公众的视线,不是在人民的欢呼中戴着花环或花冠快乐地离开的,而是在悲痛的国民的呜咽和泪水中离开的。他回家了,不是回到平

①1837～1908,美国第二十任及第二十四任总统。

15.

Eulogy of McKinley

By Grover Cleveland

Today the grave closes over the dead body of the man but lately chosen by the people of the United States from among their number to represent their nationality, preserve, protect and defend their Constitution, to faithfully execute the laws ordained for their welfare, and safely to hold and keep the honor and integrity of the Republic. His time of service is ended, not by the expiration of time, but by the tragedy of assassination. He has passed from public sight, not joyously bearing the garlands and wreaths of his countrymen´s approving acclaim, but amid the sobs and tears of a mourning nation. He has gone to his home, not the habitation of earthly peace and quiet, bright with

和安静、舒适温馨的人间住宅，而是去黑暗狭窄的,作为人们最终归宿的住所安息了,直到东方闪烁起复活的晨光。

全国人民都爱他们刚刚逝去的总统。他仁慈宽厚的天性以及善解人意、温柔体贴的性格会永远留在人民的记忆中。他也同样用他的爱国精神和无私奉献的精神爱着人民，在他们悲伤与屈辱的时刻,他常会说:“这是上帝的意志。我很满足。如果我有这样一个生死关头的教训，那就让它来教育所有仍然活着并且掌握着国家命运的人吧。”

逝去的人已经安葬，我们再也见不到他的身影，那么让我们探讨一下逝者的一生带给我们的教训和警示吧。

我首先想到的是那些构成我们大学学生主体的青年人，他们应该从麦金利的经历中吸取哪些教训。这些教训并不是晦涩难懂的,它们教育青年人珍惜学习和智力训练的价值，它更教育大家要记住只有那些品质好、素质高的人才会找到成才与成功之路并且沿着它走下去,否则便会错过它、失掉机会。而这一点经常在大学中被忽视或漠视。这是一个很大的错误。要认真地、努力地学习,但

domestic comfort and joy, but to the dark and narrow house appointed for all the sons of men, there to rest until the morning light of the resurrection shall gleam in the East.

All our people loved their dead president. His kindly nature and lovable traits of character and his amiable consideration for all about him will long be in the minds and hearts of his countrymen. He loved them in return with such patriotism and unselfishness that in the hour of their grief and humiliation he would say to them: "It is God's will; I am content. If there is a lesson in my life or death, let it be taught to those who still live and have the destiny of their country in their keeping."

Let us, then, as our dead is buried out of our sight, seek for the lessons and the admonitions that may be suggested by the life and death which constitute our theme.

First in my thoughts are the lessons to be learned from the career of William McKinley by the young men who make up the student body of our university. These lessons are not obscure or difficult. They teach the value of study and mental training, but they teach more impressively that the road to usefulness and to the only success worth having, will be missed or lost except it is sought and kept by the light of those qualities of heart, which it is sometimes supposed may safely be neglected or subordinated in university surroundings. This is a great mistake. Study and study hard, but never let the thought enter your

千万不要认为仅仅通过努力学习或仅仅储备大量的书本知识就会让你走进成才和成功的殿堂。

全国人民今天哀悼的这个人获得了伟大的祖国所能给予的最高荣誉，他的一生是有意义的一生。他有着良好的教育背景，等一会儿我会说到他辉煌的事业、他为祖国和人民所作的贡献，但是大家不会听到我说他所取得的职位和获得的成就要完全归功于他受到的教育。与此相反，我会频频提到他之所以获得了巨大成功是因为他是一个孝顺、体贴的儿子，爱国、忠诚的战士，诚实、正直的公民，温柔、忠实的丈夫，是因为他在生活的各个方面都是一个真诚、大度、无私、高尚、廉洁的人。他并不认为自己有有失男子汉气概之处。他想得很对。他是位非常杰出、非常伟大、非常有价值的人。他之所以杰出、伟大、有价值，是因为他拥有并保持了好品质、高素养。而我却担心，现在的大学生有时会认为这样的品德要求无足轻重或将之丢在脑后。

我们已故总统的死亡悲剧给了我们一个十分惨痛的教训。这个教训给了我们极大的震撼，此时此刻我简直难以平静地述说这个教训。但是我们可以看到在谋杀者血腥行为背后那些可怕的身影和令人恐怖的面孔，我们不应对此视而不见。如果

mind that study alone or the greatest possible accumulation of learning alone will lead you to the heights of usefulness and success.

The man who is universally mourned today achieved the highest distinction which his great country can confer on any man, and he lived a useful life. He was not deficient in education, but with all you will hear of his grand career, and of his services to his country and his fellow citizens, you will not hear that either the high place he reached or what he accomplished was due entirely to his education. You will instead constantly hear as accounting for his great success that he was obedient and affectionate as a son, patriotic and faithful as a soldier, honest and upright as a citizen, tender and devoted as a husband, and truthful, generous, unselfish, moral and clean in every relation of life. He never thought any of these things too weak for manliness. Make no mistake. Here was a most distinguished man, a great man, a useful man—who became distinguished, great and useful, because he had, and retained unimpaired, the qualities of heart which I fear university students sometimes feel like keeping in the background or abandoning.

There is a most serious lesson for all of us in the tragedy of our late president's death. The shock of it is so great that it is hard at this time to read this lesson calmly. We can hardly fail to see, however, behind the bloody deed of the assassin, horrible figures and faces from which it will not do to turn away. If we are to escape

我们想让和平与安全免受攻击，我们一定要勇敢地、坚定不移地与无政府主义的恶魔作斗争。这不是我们可以放心地留给哪个政党和党派去解决的问题。没有什么可以保证我们不受到它的威胁，除非我们对公民进行好品德的教育并要求公民去具体表现，除非我们彻底地揭露对社会秩序不满者和仇恨者的信条和目的，除非我们勇敢地制定和执行强硬的法律。

我们的高等院校不能不投入到反无政府主义倾向的战斗中去。他们可以帮助揭露邪恶团体和流血事件的联系并提醒人们提高警惕，他们还可以对不安定因素施加一定的影响，这些都有着不可估量的价值。

为了纪念我们遇刺的总统，让我们下决心去培养并保持那些使他伟大和有益人民的品质，让我们下定决心在祖国危难和需要的时候随时响应爱国义务的号召。

further attack upon our peace and security, we must boldly and resolutely grapple with the monster of anarchy. It is not a thing that we can safely leave to be dealt with by party or partizanship. Nothing can guarantee us against its menace except the teaching and the practise of the best citizenship, the exposure of the ends and aims of the gospel of discontent and hatred of social order, and the brave enactment and execution of repressive laws.

Our universities and colleges can not refuse to join in the battle against the tendencies of anarchy. Their help in discovering and warning against the relationship between the vicious councils and deeds of blood, and their unsteadying influence upon the elements of unrest, can not fail to be of inestimable value.

By the memory of our murdered president, let us resolve to cultivate and preserve the qualities that made him great and useful; and let us determine to meet the call of patriotic duty in every time of our country's danger or need.

16.

美国阵亡将士纪念日

托马斯·希金森[1]

朋友们:

今天，我们相聚在这儿的目的是举行没有伤心只有尊严和温柔的悼念仪式。这不是为新近失去的亲人而举行的葬礼，我们来到这里举行的是一个温和的仪式。我们不是聚集在一个新掘开的坟墓前，而是在一些已经被大自然用自己爱的纪念品装饰过的墓群中间。每座坟墓每天都感受着大自然阳光的微笑和泪水的洗礼。大自然让草儿在简陋的坟墓上安家，让藤儿在上面攀爬，让蝴蝶（古老的不朽的象征）在草地上曼舞。大自然体现了温柔，我们也要表达自己的温柔。不是“你悲我泣，你哀我伤”，而是为鲜花捧上鲜花，在桂冠上再

①1823～1911 作家，废奴主义者及军人。

16.

Decoration Day

By Thomas W. Higginson

Friends:

We meet today for a purpose that has the dignity and the tenderness of funeral rites without their sadness. It is not a new bereavement, but one which has softened, that brings us here. We meet not around a newly opened grave, but among those which Nature has already decorated with the memorials of her love. Above every tomb her daily sunshine has smiled, her tears have wept; over the humblest she has bidden some grasses nestle, some vines creep, and the butterfly,—ancient emblem of immortality—waves his little wings above every sod. To Nature's signs of tenderness we add our own. Not "ashes to ashes, dust to dust," but

加上桂冠。

伟大的南北战争已经结束了，庞大的军队裁掉了，部队的帐篷拆除了，营地的篝火熄灭了，战士的花名册闲置了。但是还有另外一支部队不会因总统公告而裁员，不会因将军命令而解散。这里就是他们的营地，这些白色的石碑就是他们的帐篷，我们所铭记的名单就是他们的花名册，他们的营火就燃烧在我们的心里。

我还记得原先的“甜蜜的奥本山”，那时还没有任何神圣的联想使它更甜美，山上的树俯视的不是这些坟墓，而是那些小鸟和蜜蜂。从那时起，时间逐渐丰富了它的记忆。尤其是在那场伟大的战争中，国家的男人好像越来越少，而这些山给人的联想却越来越丰富，直到这座墓地收纳了那个在差不多是最后一场战斗中倒下的英雄男孩。如今那本阵亡将士名册已经合上最后一页，纪念的工作也就开始了。

不分民族、种族和宗教信仰，他们都是为祖国贡献了自己的生命。今天，不分民族、种族和宗教信仰，我们也将给所有的坟墓敬献花圈。那位年轻的罗马天主教信徒临死时大喊着：“圣母玛丽亚，原谅我！”，那位年轻的信奉新教的神学院学生生前最喜欢到这座公墓里来读书，他的遗言是不要在他的墓碑上刻任何赞美的话语，这些人生前都同样地佩戴着十字架胸坠，而今天他们也将在鲜

blossoms to blossoms, laurels to the laureled.

The great Civil War has passed by—its great armies were disbanded, their tents struck, their camp-fires put out, their muster-rolls laid away. But there is another army whose numbers no Presidential proclamation could reduce, no general orders disband. This is their camping-ground—these white stones are their tents—this list of names we bear is their muster-roll—their camp-fires yet burn in our hearts.

I remember this "Sweet Auburn" when no sacred associations made it sweeter, and when its trees looked down on no funerals but those of the bird and the bee. Time has enriched its memories since those days. And especially during our great war, as the Nation seemed to grow impoverished in men, these hills grow richer in associations, until their multiplying wealth took in that heroic boy who fell in almost the last battle of the war. Now that roll of honor has closed, and the work of commemoration begun.

Without distinction of nationality, of race, of religion, they gave their lives to their country. Without distinction of religion, of race, of nationality, we garland their graves today. The young Roman Catholic convert who died exclaiming "Mary! pardon!" and the young Protestant theological student, whose favorite place of study was this cemetery, and who asked only that no words of praise might be engraven on his stone—these bore alike the cross in their lifetime, and shall bear it alike in flowers today. They gave

花丛中同样佩戴着它。正是他们的牺牲保持了国家的统一,祖国将毫无差别地永远记住他们。

所以军队里上下级有别的军衔上的那点差异在这儿毫无意义。死神给所有人晋升了同样的军衔。优秀的年轻骑兵将军骑马冲入最后一次战斗时,肩上带着闪闪的将星,胸前带着致命的伤口;没有武器的中士狙击手仍随着部队在安蒂特姆作战,准备从牺牲的战友手中接过步枪,因为他自己的枪被偷走了;还有那个在同一次战斗中有着同样行为的士兵,他偷偷地离开了被派去做勤务的医院,上了前线,这些人对我们来说都同样可敬。大自然对所有人的坟墓都同样温柔,我们对他们的爱也没有丝毫的差别。

死神有多么奇妙的定身术!我们活着的人日渐衰老。自从战争结束后,年轻的人长了皱纹,年老的人添了白发。几年后,也许只有几位年迈的老兵来做这支大军行进队列的代表了。之后再过一两年,可能这几个人也会逝去。但是埋葬在这里的烈士们将永远活在我们的记忆中。他们永远不会变;在我们的记忆里,他们就像在最后那一场突击战时那样,总是那么年轻,那么生气勃勃,那么勇敢。他们将青春永驻,只有我们会渐渐变老。

死神有多么神奇的净化术!我们身边倒下的这些战士们有着不同的性格,像所有人一样,他们

their lives that we might remain one Nation, and the Nation holds their memory alike in its arms.

And so the little distinctions of rank that separated us in the service are nothing here. Death has given the same brevet to all. The brilliant young cavalry general who rode into his last action, with stars on his shoulders and his death-wound on his breast, is to us no more precious than that sergeant of sharpshooters who followed the line unarmed at Antietam, waiting to take the rifle of some one who should die, because his own had been stolen; or that private who did the same thing in the same battle, leaving the hospital service to which he had been assigned. Nature has been equally tender to the graves of all, and our love knows no distinction.

What a wonderful embalmer is death! We who survive grow daily older. Since the war closed the youngest has gained some new wrinkle, the oldest some added gray hair. A few years more and only a few tattering figures shall represent the marching files of the Grand Army; a year or two beyond that, and there shall flutter by the window the last empty sleeve. But these who are here are embalmed forever in our imaginations; they will not change; they never will seem to us less young, less fresh, less daring, than when they sallied to their last battle. They will always have the dew of their youth; it is we alone who shall grow old.

And, again, what a wonderful purifier is death! These who fell beside us varied in character; like other men, they had their strength and their

有坚强的一面，也有脆弱的一面；有优点，也有缺点。但是现在所有的污点都经过了洗礼，他们的生命结束于人生的高潮。生命的结束认可了过去的一切。他们为国捐躯，这是他们可歌可泣的记录。他们大概发现每个战场通往天堂的路都同样长短，我们今天将把同样的爱献给他们。

“什么是胜利呢？” 一位女士问惠灵顿公爵。“是除了失败以外世界上最伟大的悲剧，女士。”若没有留下来的这份温暖的兄弟情谊，从这些天我们隐忍的情感来看，甚至我们这场伟大的战争也只是一种悲剧。这场战争为我们的国家带来了和平，带来了统一、自由和平等，另外它还给你和我带来了对这些坟墓进行神圣吊祭的机会。不管这场战争使我们个人付出了怎样的代价（健康或财产），它还是给了我们回报：我们能够站在这些坟墓中间，而不必为苟活着而感到惭愧。

法国伟大的战士德拉图尔·多韦涅是一位身经百战的英雄，但他宁愿一直当普通士兵，拿破仑曾赠给他一把宝剑和正式的称号：“法国第一士兵”。他牺牲后，拿破仑下令让他生前所在的团里一直保持着他的精神，也就是每次点名的时候，都要点他的名字，他生前身旁的战友应回答：“在战场上英勇牺牲。” 在我们的记忆中有许多英雄的名字，在这块圣洁的土地上，我们同样珍藏着他们

weaknesses, their merits and their faults. Yet now all stains seem washed away; their life ceased at its climax, and the ending sanctioned all that went before. They died for their country; that is their record. They found their way to heaven equally short, it seems to us, from every battle-field, and with equal readiness our love seeks them today.

"What is a victory like?" said a lady to the Duke of Wellington. "The greatest tragedy in the world, madam, except a defeat." Even our great war would be but a tragedy were it not for the warm feeling of brotherhood it has left behind it, based on the hidden emotions of days like these. The war has given peace to the nation; it has given union, freedom, equal rights; and in addition to that, it has given to you and me the sacred sympathy of these graves. No matter what it has cost us individually—health or worldly fortunes—it is our reward that we can stand today among these graves and yet not blush that we survive.

The great French soldier, de Latour d'Auvergne, was the hero of many battles, but remained by his own choice in the ranks. Napoleon gave him a sword and the official title "The First Grenadier of France." When he was killed, the Emperor ordered that his heart should be intrusted to the keeping of his regiment—that his name should be called at every roll-call, and that his next comrade should make answer, "Dead upon the field of honor." In our memories are the names of many heroes; we treasure all their hearts in this consecrated ground, and when the name of

的精神，当点到他们的名字时，我们会在鲜花中回答："在战场上英勇牺牲。"

注：阵亡将士纪念日，在麻省坎布里奇市奥本山公墓前的演说。

each is called, we answer in flowers, "Dead upon the field of honor."

FOOTNOTE:
Delivered at Mount Auburn Cemetery, Cambridge, Mass., Decoration Day.

17.

相信人类

阿瑟·哈德利[1]

要完成一项伟大的事业，人们必须具备两个方面的条件：个人方面的条件和社交方面的条件。他自己必须是一个正直的人，他还必须相信周围人的善意和潜在价值。

我国的学者和科学工作者有时会受到指责。人们说他们对同胞的情感漠不关心。人们还说他们批评的才能比创造的才能更强，说他们大脑发达却心胸狭隘，说他们见识增加了可同情心却减少了。

①1856～1930，美国经济学家，曾担任耶鲁大学校长22年。

17.

Faith in Mankind

By Arthur T. Hadley

In order to accomplish anything great, a man must have two sides to his greatness: a personal side and a social side. He must be upright himself, and he must believe in the good intentions and possibilities of others about him.

The scholars and scientific men of the country have sometimes been reproached with a certain indifference to the feelings and sentiments of their fellow men. It has been said that their critical faculty is developed more strongly than their constructive instinct; that their brain has been nourished at the expense of their heart; that what they have gained in breadth of vision has been outweighed by a loss of human sympathy.

应该由你们来证明这些指责是错误的。应该由你们通过自己的生活和语言来表明你们信任这些和你们共同工作的人以及你们身边的人。也许这有时是一项艰难的任务。但是如果你能正确地研究历史、文学或科学,那么在别人看来十分艰难的事,也许对你来说却很简单。你常常会觉得有责任提出并不中听的意见，也就是应告诉人们要达到向往的目标是没有捷径的。这可能会使一些热心的朋友不再信任你的领导能力。头脑清醒的人往往会被指责为铁石心肠，但是如果你信任自己的同胞,虽然这样的事会暂时阻碍你,但最终会帮助你具备宽宏大量的领导者的能力。

曾经有一段时间(不久前的一段时间),人们不相信科学工作者能够指导具体的事情，他们认为无需理论家的指导他们便能做好自己的事情。谈到商业行为时，科学工作者和一向讲究实际的人常用相互不信任的眼光看待对方。只要科学工作者一直只做理论批评，那么这种不信任就将一直继续下去。而当他们开始处理应用机械学和物理学的实际问题并广泛地具体解决这些问题的时候，他们就会在现代有形的发展中成为被信任的领导者。

你们也应该用同样的方式去解决人类生活中

It is for you to prove the falseness of this charge. It is for you to show by your life and utterances that you believe in the men who are working with you and about you. There will probably be times when this is a hard task. If you have studied history or literature or science aright, some things which look large to other people will look small to you. You will frequently be called upon to give the unwelcome advice that a desired end can not be reached by a short cut; and this may cause some of your enthusiastic friends to lose confidence in your leadership. There are always times when a man who is clear-headed is reproached with being hard-hearted. But if you yourselves keep your faith in your fellow men, these things, tho they be momentary hindrances, will in the long run make for your power of Christian leadership.

There was a time, not so very long ago, when the people distrusted the guidance of scientific men in things material. They believed that they could do their business best without advice of the theorists. When it came to the conduct of business, scientific men and practical men eyed each other with mutual distrust. As long as the scientific men remained mere critics this distrust remained. When they came to take up the practical problems of applied mechanics and physics and solve them positively in a large way, they became the trusted leaders of modern material development.

It is for you to deal with the profounder

的一些深奥问题。你们应该证明你们不仅在我们国家的机械和物质发展的方面有带头作用，而且在政治、社会和精神发展方面也有带头作用。为了能做到这些，你们必须像你们的父辈带着明确的信念去解决应用科学方面的问题那样，也要带着明确的观念去解决社会问题。对于那些信任同胞、信任祖国、把对看不见的上帝的爱派生为对看得见的同胞的爱的人来说，20世纪初的岁月是有无比希望的岁月。我们早已知道人们可以通过爱同胞来学会爱上帝。同样道理，我们会发现人们也可以通过信任同伴而学会信任上帝。

注：在耶鲁大学本科生毕业典礼上讲演的结尾部分。

problems of human life in the same way. It is for you to prove your right to take the lead in the political and social and spiritual development of the country, as well as in its mechanical and material development. To do this you must take hold of these social problems with the same positive faith with which your fathers took hold of the problems of applied science. To the man who believes in his fellow men, who has faith in his country, and in whom the love of God whom he hath not seen is but an outgrowth of a love for his fellow men whom he hath seen, the opening years of the twentieth century are years of unrivaled promise. We already know that a man can learn to love God by loving his fellow men. Equally true we shall find it that a man learns to believe in God by believing in his fellow men.

FOOTNOTE:

The concluding part of a baccalaureate address to the graduating class of Yale University.

18.

华盛顿和林肯

马丁·利特尔顿[1]

美国历史上这两位伟人的性格中最突出的地方就是不会感情用事。华盛顿既能容忍杰斐逊的法国式的激进主义，又能接受汉密尔顿的英国式的保守主义。他把这两个人都请入了他的政府内阁，但从不让他们中的任何一位左右他的政策。敌人的攻击吓不倒他，朋友的恭维骗不了他。在这方面，他和林肯的杰出性格有着惊人的相似之处。

正义是照耀林肯脚下艰难人生旅途的唯一明灯；正义是晚上使他安眠的唯一信念；正义是他用

①1872～1934，曾任美国众议院纽约州议员，达拉斯市地方检察官。

18.

Washington and Lincoln

By Martin W. Littleton

The strongest thing about the character of the two greatest men in American history is the fact that they did not surrender to the passion of the time. Washington withstood the French radicalism of Jefferson and the British conservatism of Hamilton. He invited each of them into his cabinet; he refused to allow either of them to dictate his policy. His enemies could not terrify him by assault; his friends could not deceive him with flattery. In this respect he resembled in marked degree the splendid character of Lincoln.

The single light that led Lincoln's feet along the hard highway of life was justice; the single thought that throbbed his brain to sleep at night

心灵的力量和意图轻声祈祷的唯一愿望，正义是在他那颗为祖国的悲痛而悲痛的心中绵绵不绝的唯一搏动；他感人的讲演中说出的每个字都透露出忧郁和严肃的正义精神。当整个民族因情绪激动而情绪不稳时，他处在风口浪尖上，背叛、违法，不公正、罪恶、贪污等万千不义行为有组织地或单独地压在这个忧郁的伟人肩上。当正义的心灵同罪恶开战时，当坚强的精神抵抗不公正的伤害时，当真正勇敢的心反击怯懦小人的偷袭时，这位容忍与和平的王子默默地承受着他渴望护佑的国人对他的中伤。

林肯照亮了从小木屋到白宫的路。在寂静的树林里不停地工作时，他听到过暴风雨低沉的吼声；在树叶闪光、栎树枝繁叶茂的森林里辛勤地劳作时，他就听到过列克星敦对萨姆特的呼唤、瓦利福奇对葛底斯堡的呼唤、约克敦对阿波马托克斯的呼唤。徘徊在简陋的小木屋中奄奄一息的炉火旁，他怀着悲愤的心情看到了弗吉尼亚篝火熊熊的营地，感受到了沉睡的军营中威严的寂静。透过这些，他看到的是奴隶身上绷紧的肌肉，农奴沮丧的情绪和禁锢着不朽的灵魂的枷锁。透过悲痛欲绝的泪水，向更远处望去，他还看到倚在空椅子旁边的寡妇，看到老父亲在门口徒劳的守望，看到女儿在门旁忧郁的渴盼，看到儿子迈着沉重的脚步

was justice; the single prayer that put in whispered words the might and meaning of his soul was justice; the single impulse that lingered in a heart already wrung by a nation's grief was justice; in every word that fell from him in touching speech there was the sad and sober spirit of justice. He sat upon the storm when the nation shook with passion. Treason, wrong, injustice, crime, graft, a thousand wrongs in system and in single added to the burden of this melancholy spirit. Silently, as the soul of the just makes war on sin; silently, as the spirit of the mighty withstands the spite of wrong; silently, as the heart of the truly brave resists the assault of the coward, this prince of patience and peace endured the calumny of the country he died to save.

Lincoln blazed the way from the cabin to the crown; working away in the silence of the woods, he heard the murmur of a storm; toiling in the forest of flashing leaf and armored oak, he heard Lexington calling unto Sumter, Valley Forge crying unto Gettysburg, and Yorktown shouting unto Appomattox. Lingering before the dying fires in a humble hut, he saw with sorrowful heart the blazing camps of Virginia, and felt the awful stillness of slumbering armies. Beneath it all he saw the strained muscles of the slave, the broken spirit of the serf, the bondage of immortal souls; and beyond it all, looking through the tears that broke from a breaking heart, he saw the widow by the empty chair, the aged father's fruitless vigil at the gate, the daughter's dreary watch beside the door,

从童年步入老年。在这幅画面的后面，他还看到的是在凄凉的家庭供桌上供着的香火，那是用无数破碎的心中流淌出来的泪水制成的一炷炷香。更远处，他看到的是战场，静静的墓碑无声地诉说着英勇的牺牲者的故事。他看到在荒芜的大地上沃土已经不再长出金黄的谷穗和饱满的麦穗；他看到南方冒烟的烟囱，荒寂的家园；看到伤残的人们弯着腰，低着头跋涉在回家的路上，回家后他们仍然要受穷、要消瘦、要挣扎、要重建家园；他看见北方正在从战争严重的破坏中恢复，重新连通被残酷的战争之剑切断的贸易干线。在他为国献身的一生中，他最后的一个行动是用他温柔的手击碎了战争贪婪的嘴边那可恶的装满兄弟鲜血的酒杯，并消灭了大炮的吼声，将它变成了歌曲无名的音符。

然后，我们再看看华盛顿离开平静富足的种植园，奔向那血迹斑斑的战场的情景；他放弃了作为弗吉尼亚的富绅所拥有的产业，接受了不公平的战争带给他的贫困。这是爱国主义战胜了贪婪的画面。

啊！我亲爱的朋友们，我们必须生活下去，这样才能使他们的精神留在我们的生命和行为中，

and the son's solemn step from boyhood to old age. And behind this picture he saw the lonely family altar upon which was offered the incense of tears coming from millions of broken hearts; and looking still beyond he saw the battle-fields where silent slabs told of the death of those who died in deathless valor. He saw the desolated earth, where golden grain no more broke from the rich, resourceful soil, where the bannered wheat no longer rose from the productive earth; he saw the South with its smoking chimneys, its deserted hearthstones, its maimed and wounded trudging with bowed heads and bent forms back to their homes, there to want and to waste and to struggle and to build up again; he saw the North recover itself from the awful shock of arms and start anew to unite the arteries of commerce that had been cut by the cruel sword of war. And with this gentle hand, and as a last act of his sacrificial life, he dashed the awful cup of brother's blood from the lustful lip of war and shattered the cannons' roar into nameless notes of song.

Then turn to the vision of Washington leaving a plantation of peace and plenty to suffer on the blood-stained battle-field, surrendering the dominion over the princely domain of a Virginia gentleman to accept the privations of an unequal war—the vision of patriotism over against the vision of greed.

Oh, my friends, we must live so that the spirit of these men shall settle all about our lives and deeds; so that the patriotism of their service

这样他们为民族作奉献的爱国主义精神才能成为所有追随者心中燃烧的火焰。华盛顿制定的宪法与林肯促成的全国人民的自由，应该植入我们的心中，从而让它们作为习俗世代相传，这样我们的政体才不会灭亡，我们才能为保卫国家而流尽最后一滴血；我们将把国旗看作他们无私生命的美丽象征，旗上的红色出自战士的心脏，白色是民族的泪水漂白的，星星悬挂在上面同声歌唱，直到全世界都获得自由时的永恒黎明的来临。

注：在纽约州布法罗市埃利科特俱乐部举办的华盛顿诞辰纪念日上的讲演，此为节选。

shall burn as a fire in the hearts of all who shall follow them. The Constitution which came from one, the universal liberty which came from the other, must be set in our hearts as institutions in the blood of our race, so that this Government shall not perish until every drop of that blood has been shed in its defense; and we shall behold the flag of our country as the beautiful emblem of their unselfish lives, whose red ran out of a soldier's heart, whose white was bleached by a nation's tears, whose stars were hung there to sing together until the eternal morning when all the world shall be free.

FOOTNOTE:

Extract from an address on the occasion of the celebration of Washington's Birthday by the Ellicott Club of Buffalo, New York.

19.

华盛顿的特点

威廉·麦金利①

同胞们：

有一种特别而温柔的情感与这座纪念碑相连。它不仅表达了生者的感激和崇敬，更证明了英烈的感情和敬意。

华盛顿的战友们设计了这座纪念碑。这是他们爱的作品。他们的捐助促成了它的建造。如果说历史和现在联手完成了这一工程，那么未来的后代将会从中受益。能参加这样一座纪念碑的揭幕式可谓荣幸之至。每一座华盛顿纪念碑都是爱国主义的颂歌。纪念他的每一个塔碑、每一尊雕像都有益于传授爱国精神、鼓励忠诚和弘扬更完善的

①1843～1901，第25任美国总统。

19.

Characteristics of Washington

By William McKinley

Fellow Citizens:

There is a peculiar and tender sentiment connected with this memorial. It expresses not only the gratitude and reverence of the living, but is a testimonial of affection and homage from the dead.

The comrades of Washington projected this monument. Their love inspired it. Their contributions helped to build it. Past and present share in its completion, and future generations will profit by its lessons. To participate in the dedication of such a monument is a rare and precious privilege. Every monument to Washington is a tribute to patriotism. Every shaft and statue to his memory helps to inculcate love of country,

民权。上帝保佑每一项唤起爱国主义而谴责冷漠和违法的事业！严谨地研究华盛顿的经历反而能提高我们对他多方面的伟大才干的敬重。

从独立战争爆发到宣告和平，华盛顿一直担任殖民军总司令;作为大陆会议主席,他主持会议制定了美国宪法,作为宪法下的美国第一任总统，他有着与美国其他所有杰出人物不同的荣誉。因为除了他,没有人能够和美国政体有这种关系。不仅我们民族的独立有赖于他的军事天才（他的毅力、睿智、勇气和本领）,而且在起草引导国家的宪法这件伟业中他也起到了巨大作用；他是人民选来运作新政体的第一任总统。他之所以能够赢得人民的支持、博得他们的信任,并不是因为其骄人的军事才能和令人陶醉的演说，而是因为他能冷静沉着地判断、能唤起他们高尚的抱负。而且华盛顿从来都十分谦逊，因此在他的一生中他从未有过盛气凌人的态度。他淡薄权力,不搞至尚至尊。他的荣誉都是人民给予的。

一个有趣的事实（也是我喜欢回忆的事实）

encourage loyalty and establish a better citizenship. God bless every undertaking which revives patriotism and rebukes the indifferent and lawless! A critical study of Washington's career only enhances our estimation of his vast and varied abilities.

As Commander-in-chief of the Colonial armies from the beginning of the war to the proclamation of peace, as president of the convention which framed the Constitution of the United States, and as the first President of the United States under that Constitution, Washington has a distinction differing from that of all other illustrious Americans. No other name bears or can bear such a relation to the Government. Not only by his military genius—his patience, his sagacity, his courage, and his skill—was our national independence won, but he helped in largest measure to draft the chart by which the Nation was guided; and he was the first chosen by the people to put in motion the new Government. His was not the boldness of martial display or the charm of captivating oratory, but his calm and steady judgment won men's support and commanded their confidence by appealing to their best and noblest aspirations. And withal Washington was ever so modest that at no time in his career did his personality seem in the least intrusive. He was above the temptation of power. He spurned any suggested crown. He would have no honor which the people did not bestow.

An interesting fact—and one which I love to

是在这座城市华盛顿主持召开过多次宪法会议，但他在那些会议上做过一次正式演讲，在那次演讲中他呼吁众议院增加人民代表的数量，这一呼吁立刻受到了关注。他总在热切地关注人民的权利，而那时也如现在一样，掌握着我们国家命运的是人民。

他作战时运筹帷幄，他的政府管理同样让他赢得了尊重。他的远见卓识令人钦佩；他的行政管理理念开明，他坚持认为教育、道德和文明的民权是国家的发展和长治久安所必不可少的。即使在今天，我们反思这些时，仍然为他深刻的见地和开阔的视野所震撼。他对政体的问题看得很远。他关注的不仅仅是当时，后人的利益才是他思考的永恒的主题。他开辟了自由之路。他为软弱且支离破碎的殖民地政府奠定了成长为一个统一共和国的基础。这个共和国的领土、政权、人民的自由权利已经成为世界所羡慕的对象。斗转星移，他的名声和威望丝毫未减；他的人生和成就的辉煌依然光芒万丈。伟大的行为不会停止其前进的脚步，华盛顿的丰功伟绩将被世世代代发扬光大。

recall—is that the only time Washington formally addrest the Constitutional Convention during all its sessions over which he presided in this city, he appealed for a larger representation of the people in the National House of Representatives, and his appeal was instantly heeded. Thus was he ever keenly watchful of the rights of the people in whose hands was the destiny of our Government then as now.

Masterful as were his military campaigns, his civil administration commands equal admiration. His foresight was marvelous; his conception of the philosophy of government, his insistence upon the necessity of education, morality, and enlightened citizenship to the progress and permanence of the Republic, can not be contemplated even at this period without filling us with astonishment at the breadth of his comprehension and the sweep of his vision. His was no narrow view of government. The immediate present was not his sole concern, but our future good his constant theme of study. He blazed the path of liberty. He laid the foundation upon which we have grown from weak and scattered Colonial governments to a united Republic whose domains and power as well as whose liberty and freedom have become the admiration of the world. Distance and time have not detracted from the fame and force of his achievements or diminished the grandeur of his life and work. Great deeds do not stop in their growth, and those of Washington will expand in influence in all the centuries to follow.

华盛顿留给人类文明的丰富遗产无法估量。他放在人类肩上的责任是神圣而庄严的；他留给美国人民继承和发扬其事业的义务既艰巨又严正。让我们感到高兴的是，不断有新的迹象表明人民已经清楚地认识到自己真正喜欢和怀念的是革命史上杰出的英雄们，是他们的英勇与牺牲缔造了我们的国家。他们活在我们的心中，记住他们将有助于我们信守宪法，以维护世界上最自由的政体。

我们的国家与华盛顿的名字密不可分。两者都光荣而成功。华盛顿活在我们心中，而且将流芳百世。因为他的所作所为是为了人类的进步、道德心的推崇和民主政府的建立。因此，只要我们坚持华盛顿所教导、林肯所弘扬的不朽的原则，我们的民族终将跨越千难万险而万古长青。

注：美国第24任总统威廉·麦金利在费城辛辛那提协会组织的华盛顿雕塑揭幕式上所做的演讲。

The bequest Washington has made to civilization is rich beyond computation. The obligations under which he has placed mankind are sacred and commanding. The responsibility he has left for the American people to preserve and perfect what he accomplished is exacting and solemn. Let us rejoice in every new evidence that the people realize what they enjoy and cherish with affection the illustrious heroes of Revolutionary story whose valor and sacrifices made us a nation. They live in us, and their memory will help us keep the covenant entered into for the maintenance of the freest Government of the earth.

The Nation and the name of Washington are inseparable. One is linked indissolubly with the other. Both are glorious, both triumphant. Washington lives and will live because what he did was for the exaltation of man, the enthronement of conscience, and the establishment of a Government which recognizes all the governed. And so, too, will the Nation live victorious over all obstacles, adhering to the immortal principles which Washington taught and Lincoln sustained.

FOOTNOTE:
Address by William McKinley, twenty-fourth President of the United States, delivered at the unveiling of the Washington Statue, by the Society of Cincinnati, in Philadelphia.

20.

“让法兰西自由吧！”

乔治·雅克·丹东[①]

呈现在大家眼前的基本战况是真实的；不过，此刻我们没有太大的必要去调查使我们受害的这场灾难的原因，而是要迅速采取补救措施。当大楼着火时，我没有跟那些恶棍一起去偷家具，而是去灭火。因此，我要告诉大家，你们应该相信迪穆列送来的急件，要刻不容缓地去拯救法兰西共和国。

迪穆列设想过一个充分展露他才华的方案。现在我比前不久对他更为欣赏、更为称赞有加。就在三个月前，他曾向执行权力机构，即最高国防委

①1759～1794，法国大革命早期的领军人物，第一届法国公安委员会主席。

20.

"Let France Be Free!"

By George Jacques Danton

The general considerations that have been presented to you are true; but at this moment it is less necessary to examine the causes of the disasters that have struck us than to apply their remedy rapidly. When the edifice is on fire, I do not join the rascals who would steal the furniture, I extinguish the flames. I tell you therefore you should be convinced by the despatches of Dumouriez that you have not a moment to spare in saving the Republic.

Dumouriez conceived a plan which did honor to his genius. I would render him greater justice and praise than I did recently. But three months ago he announced to the executive power, your

员会说明，倘若我们不敢在隆冬进攻荷兰，也没有胆量立刻向英国宣战（事实上，我们一直在与英国作战），那么我们的仗会打得加倍的困难，因为我们会给敌人留出部署兵力的时间。由于我们那时没有重视迪穆列这天才的一着，所以现在必须采取亡羊补牢之策。

迪穆列并未泄气；他现在在荷兰中部，在那儿他会找到军火；要击败全部敌人，他缺少的只是法兰西人，而法兰西人遍布法兰西各个角落。我们会自由吗？倘若我们已不再渴望自由，那么就让我们灭亡吧，因为我们都曾发过这样的誓言；倘若我们依然渴望自由，那么大家就应该出征以捍卫我们的独立。你们的敌人在拼死做最后一搏。皮特知道他要捍卫的是自己的全部所有，因而他敢于不惜一切代价。攻克荷兰，消灭迦太基，那么英国就除了自由之外已无路可走！就让荷兰在自由面前屈服吧；虽然目前英国的商业贵族控制着英国人民，但是连这些贵族也想起来反抗其政府，因为是政府把他们拖入了这场针对一个自由民族的残暴战争。他们终将推翻愚蠢的英国内阁，因为它竟然认为旧有的政治体制会窒息法兰西的自由骄子。一旦由于商业的利益内阁被推翻，自由党将拨云见日；因为自由党没有消亡！如果你们晓得自己的责任，如果你们的长官即刻出发，如果你们助那些渴

General Committee of Defense, that if we were not audacious enough to invade Holland in the middle of winter, to declare instantly against England the war which actually we had long been making, that we would double the difficulties of our campaign, in giving our enemies the time to deploy their forces. Since we failed to recognize this stroke of his genius we must now repair our faults.

Dumouriez is not discouraged; he is in the middle of Holland, where he will find munitions of war; to overthrow all our enemies, he wants but Frenchmen, and France is filled with citizens. Would we be free? If we no longer desire it, let us perish, for we have all sworn it. If we wish it, let all march to defend our independence. Your enemies are making their last efforts. Pitt, recognizing he has all to lose, dares spare nothing. Take Holland, and Carthage is destroyed and England can no longer exist but for Liberty! Let Holland be conquered to Liberty; and even the commercial aristocracy itself, which at the moment dominates the English people, would rise against the government which had dragged it into this despotic war against a free people. They would overthrow this ministry of stupidity who thought the methods of the *ancien régime* could smother the genius of Liberty breathing in France. This ministry once overthrown in the interests of commerce the party of Liberty would show itself; for it is not dead! And if you know your duties, if your commissioners leave at once, if you extend the

望推翻一切专制制度的陌生勇士们一臂之力，法兰西就有救了，世界就自由了。

因此，你们的长官动作要快；你们要竭力支持他们；他们最好今夜就出发。

让他们告诉那些富豪阶层的人们，欧洲的贵族阶级定会败在我们的手下，一定要让他们偿还欠债，否则你们就得偿付！法兰西人民只有血肉之躯——他们总是任人宰割！让那些忘恩负义的贵族老爷们去挥霍无度吧！瞧，公民们，光明的前程就在眼前。啊！整个民族就是你们手中有力的杠杆，民族的理智就是其支点，而你们却还没有撬起这个世界！欲达此目的，我们需要坚定、需要骨气，可惜我们很缺乏。我把一切激情搁在一边。因为除了对民众利益的激情，其他的喜怒哀乐对我来说都很陌生。

在那形势最严峻的时候，敌人就在巴黎城外，我曾对政府要员说："你们的争论实在丢人，我所看到的只是敌人。我受够了，你们不去捍卫共和国的安全，却在喋喋不休地争吵！我要断绝与你们这些卖国贼的关系！我看你们全是一路货！"我还说："我不在乎自己的名誉！让法兰西自由吧，即使我的名字会被人诅咒！就是叫我'饮血者'我也决不介意！"好啦，如果必要的话，就让我们去喝人类敌人的血；可是我们一定要战斗，一定要拥有自由。有人担心长官的出发可能会影响国民大会某些部分的职能。徒劳的担心！长官们，把你们的活力带

hand to the strangers aspiring to destroy all forms of tyranny, France is saved and the world is free.

Expedite, then, your commissioners; sustain them with your energy; let them leave this very night, this very evening.

Let them say to the opulent classes, the aristocracy of Europe must succumb to our efforts, and pay our debt, or you will have to pay it! The people have nothing but blood—they lavish it! Go, then, ingrates, and lavish your wealth! See, citizens, the fair destinies that await you. What! You have a whole nation as a lever, its reason as your fulcrum, and you have not yet upturned the world! To do this we need firmness and character, and of a truth we lack it. I put to one side all passions. They are all strangers to me save a passion for the public good.

In the most difficult situations, when the enemy was at the gates of Paris, I said to those governing: "Your discussions are shameful, I can see but the enemy. You tire me by squabbling in place of occupying yourselves with the safety of the Republic! I repudiate you all as traitors to our country! I place you all in the same line!" I said to them: "What care I for my reputation! Let France be free, tho my name were accurst! What care I that I am called 'a blood-drinker!'" Well, let us drink the blood of the enemies of humanity, if needful; but let us struggle, let us achieve freedom. Some fear the departure of the commissioners may weaken one or the other section of this Convention. Vain fears! Carry your energy

往四面八方吧。人民接到的最满意的公告将是压在他们身上的血债要由敌人来偿还，或者说富豪们很快就得偿还血债。国家形势严峻。货币不再在流通中保持平衡。工人们的劳动时间被无端延长。必须采取有力的矫正措施！荷兰的征服者正在英国扶植共和党；冲啊，法兰西，我们将让后代为我们感到光荣。奔向这些崇高的目标；不要再争辩，不要再争吵，那么祖国就有救了。

注：关于边境告急的演说——发表于国民大会。

everywhere. The pleasantest declaration will be to announce to the people that the terrible debt weighing upon them will be wrested from their enemies or that the rich will shortly have to pay it. The national situation is cruel. The representatives of value are no longer in equilibrium in the circulation. The day of the workingman is lengthened beyond necessity. A great corrective measure is necessary! Conquerors of Holland reanimate in England the Republican party; let us advance, France, and we shall go glorified to posterity. Achieve these grand destinies; no more debates, no more quarrels, and the fatherland is saved.

FOOTNOTE:

On the disasters on the frontier–delivered in convention.

21.

哈佛之子

查尔斯·德文斯[1]

哈佛之子在战争中和灾难里为国效力，感谢万能的上帝，在战斗中佑护他们，让他们能够再次站在这些古老的大厅里，站在蓊郁的树木下，这些大厅，这些树给莘莘学子留下了无数的青春与笃学的回忆；更要感谢基督仁慈地让我们的军队彻底平息了叛乱，使他们今天得以重返家园。他们所学的是和平生活的本领，并不精通战争之术，然而，在民族危难之际，他们却不得不拿起武器。

他们声称自己只是尽力履行了职责，他们来

①1820～1891，美国政治家，法学家，美国南北战争期间联合军将军。

21.

Sons of Harvard

By Charles Devens

The sons of Harvard who have served their country on field and flood, in deep thankfulness to Almighty God, who has covered their heads in the day of battle and permitted them to stand again in these ancient halls and under these leafy groves, sacred to so many memories of youth and learning, and in yet deeper thankfulness for the crowning mercy which has been vouchsafed in the complete triumph of our arms over rebellion, return home today. Educated only in the arts of peace, unlearned in all that pertained especially to the science of war, the emergency of the hour threw upon them the necessity of grasping the sword.

Claiming only that they have striven to do

这里出席这个盛大的招待会只是要与大家分享胜利的喜悦和幸福。他们记得眼前的人；今天聚集在此的一大批哈佛学子全都曾为这光荣的胜利不遗余力；那些有钱的人慷慨解囊，给政府提供了军费并且救助了各地饱受战争苦难的人们；那些虽财力不足却爱国心很强的人通过上千种途径付出了自己的时间、关注、感情和爱；在座的还有政治家和议员们，他们提出的明智的忠告和表现出的坚定的态度使我们得以安全而荣耀地来到了这里——但愿他们的任务完成得与我们一样彻底！不过，我相信他们手中的"笔的挥动不会输掉剑的厮杀所取得的胜利"，在座的诗人曾经以诸如"提尔泰奥斯号召人们准备战斗"那样火热的诗句鼓舞过我们，并且用崇高的华章激励生者、歌颂死者；在座的还有演说家，他们炽热的言语驱散了长久辩论的阴霾，然而令我们痛惜的是我们曾在漫漫长夜里常听到的那个声音却没能同我们一起迎接黎明。沉浸在对他深深的怀念里，置身于这么多作出巨大贡献的人物中，在接受你们崇高的敬意

their duty they come only to ask their share in the common joy and happiness which our victory has diffused and meet this imposing reception. When they remember in whose presence they stand; that of all the great crowd of the sons of Harvard who are here today there is not one who has not contributed his utmost to the glorious consummation; that those who have been blessed with opulence have expended with the largest and most lavish hand in supplying the government with the sinews of war and sustaining everywhere the distrest upon whom the woes of war fell; that those less large in means altho not in heart have not failed to pour out most tenderly of time and care, of affection and love, in the thousand channels that have been opened; that the statesmen and legislators whose wise counsels and determined spirit have brought us thus far in safety and honor are here,—would that their task were as completely done as ours!—yet sure I am that in their hands "the pen will not lose by writing what the sword has won by fighting;" that the poets whose fiery lyrics roused us as when "Tyrtaeus called aloud to arms," and who have animated the living and celebrated the dead in the noblest strains are here; that our orators whose burning words have so cheered the gloom of the long controversy are here, altho withal we lament that one voice so often heard through the long night of gloom was not permitted to greet with us the morning. Surrounded by memories such as his, surrounded by men such as these, we may well feel at

时，我们有理由感到你们应该得到比我们更多的敬意。当然，我们也不会忘记在座的嘉宾，他们的出席就是我们的荣耀。其中，为首的是马萨诸塞州州长阁下，他虽身着便服，却与任何士兵一样有一颗坚强的心，他曾派遣数万士兵参加这场伟大的战争；我们不应该忘记的还有已故的波托马克军队的指挥官，我们许多人曾在他的指挥下奋力作战。倘若中将的整体作战计划已表明他比荷马史诗中的英雄尤利西斯还要神圣和伟大的话，那么在扭转了葛底斯堡北部山上叛乱局面的将军面前，我们就没必要到别处去寻找阿基里斯（指敌人的致命的弱点——译者注）了。

然而，阁下，由于您要求我多介绍其他人，所以我总在谈论别人的事迹，在我看来，参加作战的哈佛之子的事迹绝对没有辜负哈佛大学。无论处在什么位置上，只要是光荣或有益的工作，他们都会承担。在科技领域，他们一直都是出类拔萃的，我们所依重的工兵大都是从这所学府习得的专业本领。医科毕业的军医凭着学识和诊断，通过手术减轻了数千伤员的痛苦。这所学府是以一位清教牧师的名义创立的，从这里毕业的牧师们也作出

receiving this noble testimonial of your regard that it is rather you who are generous in bestowing than we who are rich in deserving. Nor do we forget the guests who honor us by their presence today, chief among whom we recognize his Excellency the Governor of Massachusetts, who altho he wears the civilian's coat bears as stout a heart as beats under any soldier's jacket, and who has sent his men by the thousands and tens of thousands to fight in this great battle; and the late commanding general of the Army of the Potomac under whom so many of us have fought. If the whole and comprehensive plans of our great lieutenant-general have marked him as the Ulysses of a holier and mightier epic than Homer ever dreamed, in the presence of the great captain who fairly turned the tide of the rebellion on the hills above Gettysburg, we shall not have to look far for its Achilles.

Yet, sir, speaking always of others as you have called on me to speak for them, it seems to me that the record of the sons of the university who have served in the war is not unworthy of her. In any capacity where service was honorable or useful they have rendered it. In the departments of science they have been conspicuous and the skill of the engineer upon whom we so often depended was not seldom derived from the schools of this university. In surgery they have by learning and judgment alleviated the woes of thousands. And in the ministration of that religion in whose name this university was founded they have not been less

了不少的贡献；除了布道台上鼓舞人心的话语外，他们还赶往医院，安慰那些濒死的伤员，或者就像富勒倒在弗雷德里克斯堡一样，在两军激战的战场上献出了生命。他们都把以前所学到的原则运用到了新的环境中；不过，正如大家所记得的那样，我们之中数量最多的是军队的战斗人员，他们在参军后所表现出来的才华赢得了赞誉，这更加验证了大家一直坚持到现在的论断：我们学校是为莘莘学子提供普通高等教育的最佳学府，为他们习得高层次的有用才能打下了基础。在部队里，他们迅速掌握了军事上的战术及其他的方方面面的细节，证明了自己能够应付重大的军事问题，他们的勇气和胆识是有口皆碑的。

如果有人认为这些哈佛之子给我军增加的只是肉体力量和英勇气概的话，那么他就大错特错了。与我们隔海相望的邻居，由于对君主制情有独钟，有时便对共和制有成见，恶意攻击我军的性质和纪律。没有比这更荒谬的了。联邦军队是一支崇高、忠诚、富有自我牺牲精神的军队，哈佛之子以及像他们一样的战士为这支军队的纪律规范作出了无人可比的贡献。战争中，他们总是心怀高尚的

devoted; not only have cheering words gone forth from their pulpits, but they have sought the hospitals where the wounded were dying, or like Fuller at Fredericksburg, have laid down their lives on the field where armed hosts were contending. All these were applying the principles of their former education to new sets of circumstances; but, as you will remember, by far the larger portion of our number were of the combatants of the army, and the facility they displayed in adopting the profession of arms affords an admirable addition to the argument by which it has been heretofore maintained that the general education of our college was best for all who could obtain it, as affording a basis upon which any superstructure of usefulness might be raised. Readily mastering the tactics and detail of the profession, proving themselves able to grapple with its highest problems, their courage and gallantry were proverbial.

It would be a great mistake to suppose that all that was added to our army by such men as these was merely what it gained in physical force and manly prowess. Our neighbors on the other side of the water, whose attachment to monarchy is so strong that it sometimes makes them unjust to republics, have sometimes attacked the character and discipline of our army. Nothing could be more unjust. The federal army was noble, self-sacrificing, devoted always, and to the discipline of that army no men contributed more than the members of this university and men such as they. They bore

信念；在人际交往中，他们十分注重自己的信誉。对营地骚乱，抢劫和掠夺之类的行为，他们嫉恶如仇。他们为之战斗的事业十分神圣，他们的战袍十分洁白，他们不容许那样的行为将它玷污。

校长阁下，如果我忘记了今天的仪式不仅是为了迎接那些凯旋而归的人们，更是为了纪念那些在战争中为国捐躯的英烈们，那么我就没有履行好您的指示。最适合代表您讲话的本应是我们最早的毕业生，1883级的韦伯斯特先生，虽然他没能参加这场战争，可是他在第二次马纳萨斯战争中血染沙场，用生命实践了自己的信念，保卫了宪法的尊严，而他伟大的父亲是宪法最卓越的辩护者。今天对那些从战场上回来的人们来说，不论我们遇到过什么样的危难，我们都不能认为自己的贡献无愧于母校的慷慨教诲；但对于那些业已奉献出一生，那些与共和国缔造者的英名紧密相连的人们来说，当然，还有各地那些为自由而斗争的勇士和英烈们，我们知道无论多么高的荣誉他们都是当之无愧的。在决定胜利的最后一战中，那高喊冲锋的洪亮声音，在战斗失利时仍鼓励战士顽强坚持，不轻易后退的镇定、不屈的呼声，此刻似乎还响在我们耳边。我们和后人将总会提起他们

always with them the loftiest principle in the contest and the highest honor in all their personal relations. Disorder in camp, pillage and plunder, found in them stern and unrelenting foes. They fought in a cause too sacred, they wore a robe too white, to be willing to stain or sully it with such corruption.

Mr. President I should ill do the duty you have called on me to perform if I forgot that this ceremonial is not only a reception of those who return, but a commemoration of those who have laid down their lives for the service of the country. He who should have properly spoken for us, the oldest of our graduates, altho not of our members who have fought in this war,—Webster of the class of 1833, sealed his faith with his life on the bloody field of the second Manassas, dying for the constitution of which his great father was the noblest expounder. For those of us who return to-day, whatever our perils and dangers may have been, we can not feel that we have done enough to merit what you so generously bestow; but for those with whom the work of this life is finished and yet who live forever inseparably linked with the great names of the founders of the Republic, and not them alone, but the heroes and martyrs of liberty everywhere, we know that no honor can be too much. The voices which rang out so loud and clear upon the charging cheer that heralded the final assault in the hour of victory, that in the hour of disaster were so calm and resolute as they sternly struggled to stay the slow retreat are not

如何放弃了安逸、别离了家园，义无反顾地承担起艰辛的工作，勇敢地面对危险，慷慨地献出了生命，而这一切不是为了追名逐利，而是最崇高的自我牺牲精神和爱国主义精神的体现。今天，在这里，我们为自己是哈佛之子而感到自豪，一想起这些，我们会感到没有辜负哈佛的培养，我们不妨说，“斯巴达有许多比我们更可敬的儿子。”

注：在坎布里奇举行的校庆仪式上的演讲词。

silent yet. To us and to those who will come after us, they will speak of comfort and home relinquished, of toil nobly borne, of danger manfully encountered, of life generously surrendered and this not for pelf or ambition, but in the spirit of the noblest self–devotion and the most exalted patriotism. Proud as we who are here today have a right to be that we are the sons of this university, and not deemed unworthy of her when these are remembered, we may well say, "Sparta had many a worthier son than we."

FOOTNOTE:
Speech at Commemoration Exercises held at Cambridge.

22.

醒来吧，英格兰！

国王乔治[1]

以王后陛下和王室其他成员的名义，我谨代表我本人及王妃，真诚地感谢您，市长阁下。感谢您热情的祝酒词和慷慨的款待。您动情地提及近来我们已有很长一段时间没有和我亲爱的家人在一起了，这也表现了这个国家的人民无论是在悲伤还是喜庆的日子里对我敬爱的父母的普遍关心，我敬爱的母亲童年时就一直感受着英国人民对她的关心。而我们自己，此刻也切身体会到这种

①1865～1936，英国国王乔治五世，全名乔治·弗雷德里克·恩斯特·阿尔伯特·温沙。

22.

Wake up, England!

By King George

In the name of the Queen and the other members of my family, on behalf of the Princess and for myself, I thank you most sincerely for your enthusiastic reception of this toast, proposed by you, my Lord Mayor, in such kind and generous terms. Your feeling allusion to our recent long absence from our happy family circle gives expression to that sympathy which has been so universally extended to my dear parents, whether in times of joy or sorrow, by the people of this country, and upon which my dear mother felt she could ever reckon from the first days of her life here amongst them. As to ourselves, we are deeply sensible of the great honor done us on this

荣誉，今天伦敦市政府和人民为我们举办盛大的招待会，这让我们备受感动。我希望借此机会向同胞们对我们的行程所怀的诚心牵挂和我返回时受到的热烈欢迎，表达我最诚挚的感激之情。市长阁下，感谢您提及陛下赐予我威尔士王子的头衔作为此次回家的标志。我只希望不辜负这一有历史意义的古老头衔，因为我亲爱的父亲曾经拥有这一头衔长达 59 年。

市长阁下，您给了我们言过其实的赞誉。因为我觉得这份感激之情不是国家欠我们的，而是我们欠国王和政府的。是他们设身处地为我们着想，让我们顺利地完成了这次别具一格的旅行，使我们增长了见识，丰富了阅历；在记忆里留下了国王陛下海外隶属国的许多民族给予的热情欢迎。今天在我们伟大帝国的首都，我要再次提起在这次漫长而难忘的旅途中，我们受到的忠诚、慈爱和热烈的欢迎，这让我们深深地感动和感激。我们的旅程全长超过 45000 英里，其中 33000 英里是海路，我想你们对此一定很感兴趣吧。此外，会令所有人

occasion, and our hearts are moved by the splendid reception which today has been accorded us by the authorities and inhabitants of the City of London. And I desire to take this opportunity to express our deepest gratitude for the sympathetic interest with which our journey was followed by our fellow countrymen at home, and for the warm welcome with which we were greeted on our return. You were good enough, my Lord Mayor, to refer to his Majesty having marked our home-coming by creating me Prince of Wales. I only hope that I may be worthy to hold that ancient and historic title, which was borne by my dear father for upward of fifty-nine years.

My Lord Mayor, you have attributed to us more credit than I think we deserve. For I feel that the debt of gratitude is not the nation's to us, but ours to the King and Government for having made it possible for us to carry out, with every consideration for our comfort and convenience, a voyage unique in its character, rich in the experience gained and in memories of warm and affectionate greetings from the many races of his Majesty's subjects in his great dominions beyond the seas. And here in the capital of our great Empire I would repeat how profoundly touched and gratified we have been by the loyalty, affection and enthusiasm which invariably characterized the welcome extended to us throughout our long and memorable tour. It may interest you to know that we travelled over 45,000 miles, of which 33,000 were by sea, and I think it is a matter of which

备感自豪的是，除了塞德港，我们从未踏上过没有英国国旗飘扬的土地。 我们三月中旬离开英格兰，首先抵达直布罗陀和马耳他，在那儿，当过水兵的我很高兴遇上了直布罗陀海峡和地中海的两支了不起的舰队。穿过苏伊士运河（一座海峡对岸伟大而友好民族之子的天才和勇气的丰碑），我们进入了东方之门——亚丁港。我们稍作停留，欣赏了锡兰和马来半岛旖旎的自然风光以及当地民族多姿多彩的表演，我们还看到了在大英帝国的统治下，不同民族的人民幸福地生活在一派欣欣向荣的景象中。可能还有一个现象更引人注目，那就是这些国家的政府、商业和各种企业都是在为数不多的我们英国同胞们的领导和指导下才培养出高素质的人才，而这些人才又为我们赢得并维持了这种繁荣的景象。澳大利亚，作为我们行程的真正目标，见证了这次伟大使命的圆满完成，你们可以想象在刚刚诞生的澳大利亚联邦政府首次代表大会上，我主持开幕式时是多么自豪。澳大利亚这块岛屿大陆的命运就这样交在了联邦政府的手中，在澳大利亚我们待了好几个星期，去了不同的州，度过了一段欢乐的时光，我们得以深入了解那个国家引以为荣的商业、社会和政治机制的运行情况，看到了他们在一些方面取得的巨大进步以

all may feel proud that, with the exception of Port Said, we never set foot on any land where the Union Jack did not fly. Leaving England in the middle of March, we first touched at Gibraltar and Malta, where, as a sailor, I was proud to meet the two great fleets of the Channel and Mediterranean. Passing through the Suez Canal—a monument of the genius and courage of a gifted son of the great friendly nation across the Channel—we entered at Aden the gateway of the East. We stayed for a short time to enjoy the unrivaled scenery of Ceylon and the Malay Peninsula, the gorgeous displays of their native races, and to see in what happy contentment these various peoples live and prosper under British rule. Perhaps there was something still more striking in the fact that the Government, the commerce, and every form of enterprise in these countries are under the leadership and direction of but a handful of our countrymen, and to realize the high qualities of the men who have won and kept for us that splendid condition. Australia saw the consummation of the great mission which was the more immediate object of our journey, and you can imagine the feelings of pride with which I presided over the inauguration of the first representative Assembly of the new-born Australian Commonwealth, in whose hands are placed the destinies of the great island continent. During a happy stay of many weeks in the different States, we were able to gain an insight into the working of the commercial, social and political institutions of which the country justly

及他们极强的能力；同时我们还结识了不少热情豪放的澳大利亚朋友，其品德和干劲为上述进步提供了保障。新西兰给我们提供了一个显著的范例，让我们看到一个生机勃勃的、独立与繁荣的民族如何充分享受着自由体制下的幸福生活，那里正在尝试许多有趣的社会实验。我们还高兴地参加了毛利人的盛大聚会，他们勇敢、不屈不挠，曾经是我们的敌人，而现在则是国王陛下忠实且爱好和平的臣民。塔斯马尼亚岛独特的自然风光和气候让我们想起了英伦故园，我们最终在回程之前访问了这个州。毛里求斯有美丽的热带风光，很容易让人联想起它那古典艺术、文学和海军的历史，还有那里的人民，天生就有着古老法国的一切极具魅力的特征，这里是我们归途中停留的第一站，此后我们在纳塔尔和开普殖民地上，受到了特别热烈的欢迎，考虑到那里的人民曾经长期遭受残酷的战争磨难，这欢迎显得尤为隆重。继澳大利亚和新西兰之后，我们又把祖国深情感激她英勇儿女所作贡献的口信带到了加拿大。此次跨越大洋的航行，既舒适又安排得井井有条，一路上我们看到了无限美好的风光、富饶的土地以及广阔得只得到部分开发的领土上那无穷的潜力。我们也看到了把两个伟大民族融为一体的努力已经获得

boasts, and to see something of the great progress which it has already made, and of its great capabilities, while making the acquaintance of the warm-hearted and large-minded men to whose personality and energy so much of that progress is due. New Zealand afforded us a striking example of a vigorous, independent and prosperous people, living in the full enjoyment of free and liberal institutions, and where many interesting social experiments are being put to the test of experience. Here we had the satisfaction of meeting large gatherings of the Maori people—once a brave and resolute foe, now peaceful and devoted subjects of the King. Tasmania, which in natural characteristics and climate reminded us of the old country, was visited when our faces were at length turned homeward. Mauritius, with its beautiful tropical scenery, its classical, literary and naval historical associations, and its population gifted with all the charming characteristics of old France, was our first halting-place, on our way to receive, in Natal and Cape Colony, a welcome remarkable in its warmth and enthusiasm, which appeared to be accentuated by the heavy trial of the long and grievous war under which they have suffered. To Canada was borne the message—already conveyed to Australia and New Zealand—of the Motherland's loving appreciation of the services rendered by her gallant sons. In a journey from ocean to ocean, marvelous in its comfort and organization, we were enabled to see something of its matchless scenery, the richness of its soil, the boundless possibilities of

成功。 按照国王的明确旨意，我们归途中要停留的最后一站是纽芬兰，那是英国统治时间最长的殖民地，1860 年国王陛下曾首次对其进行访问。这个岛上好客的、以航海为业的居民友好地接待了我们，其热情的程度我们至今还记忆犹新。

如果有人要我讲一讲这次旅行中特别突出的印象，我马上想到的是各地人民对国王的忠诚和对故国的依恋；人们无一例外地会提到故乡，即便是那些从未来过或是永远也不可能来英伦三岛的人也是如此，这让我十分感动。这种忠诚无疑是力量意识的证明，也证明了他们是大英帝国中真正的一员，证明了他们有能力并且愿意去担负一份义务与责任。如果让我找出形成这种精神的原因的话，在很大程度上我会将其归功于已故的敬爱的女王陛下给我们的教导和榜样作用。在走访的过程中，我们发现许多民族，甚至是那些偏远地区的民族，对于她的逝去无不深感悲痛，无不深情地缅怀，这是我毫不夸张的亲见亲闻。此外，难道我们没有发现还有一个原因吗？那就是在过去的 50 年中，英国一直对自己的殖民地实行着开明的政策。正是由于母国与其殖民地的良好关系，我们才

that vast and but partly explored territory. We saw, too, the success which has crowned the efforts to weld into one community the peoples of its two great races. Our final halting–place was, by the express desire of the King, Newfoundland, the oldest of our colonies and the first visited by his Majesty in 1860. The hearty seafaring population of this island gave us a reception the cordiality of which is still fresh in our memories.

If I were asked to specify any particular impressions derived from our journey, I should unhesitatingly place before all others that of loyalty to the Crown and of attachment to the country; and it was touching to hear the invariable reference to home, even from the lips of those who never had been or were never likely to be in these islands. And with this loyalty were unmistakable evidences of the consciousness of strength; of a true and living membership in the Empire, and of power and readiness to share the burden and responsibility of that membership. And were I to seek for the causes which have created and fostered this spirit, I should venture to attribute them, in a very large degree, to the light and example of our late beloved Sovereign. It would be difficult to exaggerate the signs of genuine sorrow for her loss and of love for her memory which we found among all races, even in the most remote districts which we visited. Besides this, may we not find another cause—the wise and just policy which in the last half century has been continuously maintained toward our colonies? As a result of the

看到在南非捍卫民族尊严时他们自发地聚集于这古老的旗帜下。检阅完六万多士兵的部队后，我完全可以对澳大利亚、新西兰和加拿大的军队实力做出评判。他们的部队都是量足质优的好材料，只需要能力强、经验多的军官将其打造成才。我迫不及待地想提一提在澳大利亚和新西兰做得很扎实、值得称道的一件事——学生军训队运动。有好几次，当看到数千名接受军训的学生全副武装齐步行进时，我深感快慰；他们分别由各自的政府资助参加军事训练，有时候政府每年还提供一次实弹练习的弹药。在军队改革的今天，我只想冒昧地请我的朋友——军机大臣关注这件有趣的事情。

今天我很荣幸在这里见到了代表大英帝国商业利益的嘉宾们，冒昧地谈一谈此行中的另一个印象，那就是他们海外的同行们普遍认为，如果英国想在殖民地贸易中保持原有优势以便与外国竞争者抗衡，那么这个古老的帝国必须醒来。有幸参与这次旅行的成员无一不对一个普遍的紧急需求

happy relations thus created between the mother country and her colonies we have seen their spontaneous rally round the old flag in defense of the nation's honor in South Africa. I had ample opportunities to form some estimate of the military strength of Australia, New Zealand, and Canada, having reviewed upward of 60,000 troops. Abundant and excellent material is available, requiring only that molding into shape which can be readily effected by the hands of capable and experienced officers. I am anxious to refer to an admirable movement which has taken strong root in both Australia and New Zealand—and that is the cadet corps. On several occasions I had the gratification of seeing march past several thousand cadets, armed and equipped, and who at the expense of their respective Governments are able to go through a military course, and in some cases with an annual grant of practise ammunition. I will not presume, in these days of army reform, to do more than call the attention of my friend, the Secretary of State for War, to this interesting fact.

To the distinguished representatives of the commercial interests of the Empire, whom I have the pleasure of seeing here today, I venture to allude to the impression which seemed generally to prevail among their brethren across the seas, that the old country must wake up if she intends to maintain her old position of pre-eminence in her colonial trade against foreign competitors. No one who had the privilege of enjoying the experiences which we have had during our tour could fail to

感到吃惊，那就是对增加人口的需求。即使在那些最古老的殖民地，亦有大量的迹象表明了这种需求。广袤的区域仍无人涉足，藏在地下的矿产财富等待着开发，大片的处女地正准备着为拓荒者产出庄稼。人们可以在健康的生活、开明的法律、自由的机制有保障的条件下去那里享受新天地，这就能够摆脱英伦故国城市人口过密的问题和几乎是无望的生存斗争的问题。哎！与生存做几乎是无望的斗争常常是英伦三岛上许多人的命运啊。但我们的殖民地兄弟也提出了一个条件，一个唯一的条件，那就是，“给我们送合格的移民过来”。我想更进一步呼吁祖国的同胞们，为了展示祖国母亲对其孩子的深情，我们将把最优秀的人才送过去。只有这样我们才能进一步巩固并且原封不动地传承我们的民族自豪感、我们情感与目标的统一以及我们对忠诚和义务的共同理解，也只有把这些内涵融合在一起才能维持大英帝国的完整。

注：乔治国王在伦敦市政厅的演讲。当时还是威尔士王子的乔治国王，刚结束殖民地的旅行回国。经刊录该报告的《泰晤士报》所有人的同意收入本书。

be struck with one all-prevailing and pressing demand: the want of population. Even in the oldest of our colonies there were abundant signs of this need. Boundless tracts of country yet unexplored, hidden mineral wealth calling for development, vast expanses of virgin soil ready to yield profitable crops to the settlers. And these can be enjoyed under conditions of healthy living, liberal laws, free institutions, in exchange for the over-crowded cities and the almost hopeless struggle for existence which, alas, too often is the lot of many in the old country. But one condition, and one only, is made by our colonial brethren, and that is, "Send us suitable emigrants." I would go further, and appeal to my fellow countrymen at home to prove the strength of the attachment of the motherland to her children by sending to them only of her best. By this means we may still further strengthen, or at all events pass on unimpaired, that pride of race, that unity of sentiment and purpose, that feeling of common loyalty and obligation which knit together and alone can maintain the integrity of our Empire.

FOOTNOTE:

A speech delivered by His Majesty King George when Prince of Wales, at the Guildhall, London, on his return from his tour of the Empire. With the permission of the proprietors of The Times the report which appeared in that paper has been followed.